create jewelry
pearls

create **jewelry**
pearls

Luxurious Designs
to Make and Wear

Marlene Blessing and Jamie Hogsett | Editors of *Beadwork* magazine

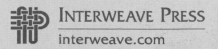

INTERWEAVE PRESS
interweave.com

Photography, Joe Coca (unless otherwise specified)

All designs, Jamie Hogsett

All narrative text, Marlene Blessing

Interweave Press LLC
201 East Fourth Street
Loveland, Colorado 80537 USA
www.interweave.com

Printed in China by C & C Offset Printing Co., Ltd.

Library of Congress Cataloging-in-Publication Data

Blessing, Marlene, 1947-
  Creating jewelry : pearls, luxurious designs to make and wear / Marlene Blessing and Jamie Hogsett, authors.
     p. cm.
  Includes index.
  ISBN 978-1-59668-023-4 (pbk.)
  1. Jewelry making. 2. Pearls. I. Hogsett, Jamie, 1978- II. Title.
  TT212.B56 2007
  739.27--dc22

                              2007001883

10 9 8 7 6 5 4 3 2 1

For Camille, artist, scientist, and luminous niece. —*MB*

For Gail Kanemoto Hogsett, Jane Kanemoto, and Karen Wood, who helped with stringing and are a constant source of love and support. —*JH*

Pearls, A Lasting Love Affair   6

Pearl Basics   8

Classic
Classic Pearl Knotting, page 18
Purple Pearls, page 22
Dark Beauties, page 24
Coin of the Realm, page 26
Mother-of-Pearl Radiance, page 28
The Midas Touch, page 32
Cuff Deluxe, page 36

Special Occasion
Champagne Necklace, page 44
Sacred Vows Lariat, page 48
Lavender Bouquet, page 52
Pearl Fusion, page 58
Copper Romance, page 62
Midnight Tassel, page 66

Fashion-Forward
Chain Reaction, page 74
Global Pearls, page 78
Catch of the Day, page 82
Off the Grid, page 86
Ocean Wonders, page 92
Wild Trellis, page 96
Center of Attention, page 98
Brilliant Bangle, page 102
Very Berry, page 106

Techniques and Findings   111

Related Reading   116

Resources   117

Index   119

pearls
A Lasting Love Affair

W E ARE DRAWN TO THE SENSUOUS BEAUTY OF A PEARL, to its soft contours, and most of all to the warm, persistent light that seems to glow from within this unique gem. Kings and queens have filled royal treasuries with them and worn impressive pearl jewelry to proclaim power and regency. Movie stars and fashion legends have greeted their public draped in glamorous pearls. Brides and debutantes have favored pearls as the gem of purity and fidelity. And the love affair continues. For those who cherish the radiance of pearls and who wish to make signature jewelry with them, we present this special collection of pearl jewelry designs. Today's affordable, varied supply of freshwater pearls is truly a beader's delight.

As you explore the beaded jewelry and the pearl lore in the pages to come, you will find beautiful designs that fit many moods and occasions. And you will come to appreciate the rich natural and human history of pearls. Accent a suit or dress with one of the **Classic** pieces, such as the multistrand mother-of-pearl necklace or the simple but elegant knotted pearl necklace. Or find the perfect jewelry for a **Special Occasion**, whether you are drawn to the baroque black pearl necklace or the diaphanous silk-ribboned necklace with wirewrapped pearls. And finally, for the times when you want to make a piece of jewelry that will express a more **Fashion-Forward** style, look to the seductive allure of hammered silver chain mixed with white, black, and teal pearls. Or create an extravaganza of varied pearl and silver charms, attached to an impressive length of braided cord.

A thrilling adventure in pearl beading awaits you, complete with clear instructions and inspiration enough to embark on your own love affair with pearls.

pearl
basics

ONE WORD will always be linked to the pearl—*luster*. We are drawn to the inner light that seems to emanate from its center. It's not just your imagination; science provides the explanation for the pearl's romance.

In cultured saltwater and freshwater pearls, an irritant is surgically implanted into the mollusk's gonad (pearl sack). The irritant or *nucleus* is either a tiny piece of mantle tissue or a combination of tissue and a tiny seed (usually a spherical bead made of mother-of-pearl). Over time, concentric layers of *nacre*, a smooth, hard substance that the mollusk secretes to protect itself, form around the nucleus. Pearls and the mother-of-pearl that coats the inside of a pearl oyster or mussel's shell are both made of nacre.

Calcium carbonate, the same material that forms shells and the skeletons of other marine creatures, is the major component in nacre. The primary form of calcium carbonate found in pearls is aragonite, a crystal. The other ingredients in nacre are organic membranes (composed of *conchiolin*) and water. The aragonite crystals are interleaved with the organic membrane in much the same way that bricks and mortar are layered, with the microscopic crystals serving as the building blocks and the conchiolin as the mortar. The very same process occurs in a natural pearl, one that has not been "assisted" by human intervention. Contrary to the popular belief that a natural pearl forms around a stray grain of sand, the intruder is more likely a tiny parasite.

In a miracle of nature, when light passes along the axis of one of these closely aligned crystals, it is reflected by others next to it and creates a pearl's characteristic luster. The more perfectly round the shape of the pearl and the more translucent the layers of nacre, the greater the degree of luster. This effect of light, color, and translucence is what makes pearls so magical in their show of silky radiance. We value a pearl not only for its size and shape, but for its radiant inner glow.

Five Basics in Choosing Pearls

Although the five criteria for selecting the best pearls—luster, surface, shape, color, and size—matter most when buying fine jewelry, they are still important when you choose pearls for your own jewelry-making. Most of all, you'll want to find pearls with the highest degree of **luster**. Look for pearls that have a deep, warm glow. These will give the richest look to your designs, no matter how simple or complex. Remember that freshwater pearls are almost pure nacre, the source of the pearl's radiance. Next, check the **surface** of pearls for scratches, cracks, spots, bumps, or other blemishes. Just as when picking an apple or pear, you want to buy pearls that are as free of flaws as possible.

Basic Pearl Necklace Lengths

Because pearls were once the exclusive province of nobles and royals (and later wealthy socialites), necklace lengths were often chosen to create the most impressive display of opulence and wealth. Thus, pearl ropes, especially in layered multiples, would signify the power of an Indian maharajah, the political clout of a ruler such as Elizabeth I, or the affluence of an industrialist's wife. More was better.

There were favored styles for various eras, such as the multistrand "dog collar" during Victorian times, opera and rope lengths for flappers in the Roaring Twenties, or the classic princess length for well-turned-out debutantes in the 1950s. Today, with the reasonable prices of cultured pearls (especially freshwater varieties), beaders can simply choose the lengths they find most fun and flattering.

Collar (12–13")

Choker (14–16")

Princess (17–19")

Matinee (20–24")

Opera (28–34")

Rope (Over 45")

The first thing you'll probably notice in a pearl is its **shape**. The most valuable pearls are perfectly round, but when making your own jewelry, you will most likely consider lots of shape options. The same is true of **color**. Traditional pearl colors include white, cream, rose, gold, blue-gray, and black. But today's cultivated pearls come in almost any shape or color, creating countless design possibilities. One important caveat: when you buy pearls that have been dyed, the color may fade or rub off. Be sure to ask the seller what to expect. And finally, **size** matters. Like most gems, the bigger the pearl, the more expensive. There are some fun exceptions—you may have seen huge, oversized round pearls in the market recently. Most of these are made of ground mother-of-pearl that is reconstituted and formed into these big pearls. The price is right on these, and they give beaders a chance to make a major pearl statement!

Dealers who sell pearls for use in beadwork sell them by the strand, so you can't really cull the strands for individual pearls. Instead, focus on selecting entire strands that seem to have the best collection of pearls.

The Soft Touch—Caring for Your Pearls

Think of a pearl's surface as being only as strong as your fingernail. A pearl is essentially alkaline in composition, which makes all acidic substances its enemy, from perfume to salad dressing. This fragile gem requires special care.

Storage: To prevent scratching the pearls' surface, avoid placing them next to jewelry or other objects with sharp edges. A silk pouch or a separate compartment in your jewelry box is the ideal storage solution for your pearls. Airtight storage, however, is not. Pearls need the moisture in the air to maintain their luster, so make sure your storage containers are porous. And do wear your pearls regularly to give them the added advantage of contact with the natural oils in your skin.

Cleaning: Don't use anything more complicated than a dry or damp soft cloth to clean pearls. If you really want to go further, you can use a bar of plain soap (not detergent) to clean the pearls in soapy water, but it's probably not necessary unless you've just doused them with salad dressing or sprayed them directly with perfume. Then you'll want to do a quick wash of your pearls to make sure the acid doesn't discolor your pearls or eat away at their surface.

Stringing/Restringing: Many beaders like to string their pearls on silk thread with a knot between each pearl, to prevent rubbing and to keep each one secure should the thread break. If you choose this classic method, you will probably need to restring and reknot your pearls every couple of years, depending on how much you wear them. Fine beading wire is another common way to string pearls. To simulate the look of tiny knots between each pearl, string a small seed bead (size 11° or smaller) between pearls.

Pearl Shapes for Beading

Virtually all of the pearls we use in making our own jewelry are cultured fresh-water pearls. These days, the market is filled with colors and shapes of all varieties, including such novelty shapes as squares, rectangles, crosses, coins, and diamonds. All it takes to produce them is the insertion of a piece of mantle tissue into the oyster or mussel, cut in the desired shape of the finished pearl.

In other words, the shape of a pearl is determined by the shape of its nucleus.

Round. Unless they are of gem quality or imitation, these are rarely perfect spheres. Round continues to reign as the classic desired shape for a pearl. However, most are actually off-round pearls, which look round but are slightly oval or flattened.

Oval. These are sometimes known as rice pearls, from the days when low-quality freshwater pearls first came onto the market and were called "rice krispies" after the cereal of that name. Today's oval pearls are quite high in quality. Some oval pearls are joined twins that grow in the same mollusk. They often have a seam in the middle.

Baroque. Pearls with irregular shapes are categorized as *baroque.* These can occur naturally in large fantastic shapes— some of the most impressive have been mounted in fine jewelry as figurative pieces—or in small forms such as Keshi pearls. The French term *baroque* originally applied to pearls, and only later was it used to categorize a style of music, art, and architecture.

Keshi. These accidental  byproducts of pearl culturing in both salt-water and freshwater mollusks are created by spontaneous nacre production in mollusks that have previously produced cultured pearls. Often called poppy or seed pearls (*Keshi* is Japanese for poppyseed), the tiny beauties are seldom round in shape and are almost always baroque.

Button. These are round on one side and flat on the other, because the pearl has attached to the shell of the mollusk.

Biwa. Also called "stick pearls," Biwas were originally named after freshwater pearls cultured in Lake Biwa near Kyoto, Japan. Industrial pollution in Japan's famous lake ended production of the pearls in 1980. Today's Biwa pearls have the name and  unique shape of the originals, although they are produced in several freshwater locales in Japan and China.

the
projects

classic

Soft spring breezes blow through the garden, carrying the fresh scent of lilac. Casting a final look around at the tables you have set, you feel satisfied. The greens, the purples and pinks, the tiny white blooms—this setting could not be more perfect for your afternoon garden party. Even the birds are adding their music to the scene.

On such a day, good food matters, table settings matter, and you, the hostess, matter. Whether you're dressing for a garden party with friends or for an important business meeting with colleagues, you want to look poised and confident. Nothing creates the impression of effortless style like a classic piece of pearl jewelry.

The ultimate timeless design is a simple knotted pearl necklace or bracelet—perhaps you recall your mother wearing a luminous strand of pearls. Simplicity and elegance characterize classic pieces, and the pearls used in them are in rich hues from creamy whites to dark grays and black, while accents of color and sparkle highlight your individuality. These designs reflect a soft glow, calling attention to you, not to themselves.

Be a vision in a simple pair of coin pearl earrings or feel radiant in a five-strand choker made of small seed pearls and Biwa. Or wrap two large strands of perfect glass pearls in rich shades of gray, blue, and black around your neck. These looks and more can be handcrafted, allowing you to make your own keepsake classics to wear again and again.

Classic Pearl Knotting

The classic strand of pearls features a knot between each pair of pearls, to protect each pearl's surface from scratching on its neighbors and to prevent a broken strand from spilling the entire necklace. White pearls strung on knotted silk to the traditional princess length are a timeless statement of elegance and distinction.

NECKLACE

36 cream 10mm Swarovski crystal
    pearls
Sterling silver toggle clasp
2 sterling silver 6mm jump rings
1 sterling silver 8mm soldered jump ring
1 package of cream size 4 Griffin Silk
    Bead Cord
1/2" of silver French wire
Hypo-cement

BRACELET

19 cream 5x7mm pearls
Sterling silver toggle clasp
1/2" of silver French wire
1 package of size 4 Griffin Silk Bead
    Cord (or remainder of silk left over
    from necklace)
Hypo-cement

TOOLS

Scissors
Tri-Cord Knotter or awl and tweezers

FINISHED SIZE

Necklace: 18" (45.5 cm)
Bracelet: 7 1/2" (18 cm)

Necklace

1 Unwrap the silk thread from the card and gently stretch it by pulling it inch by inch between your forefinger and thumb.

2 Use one 6mm jump ring to attach the bar half of the clasp to the other 6mm jump ring. Attach the second 6mm jump ring to the 8mm soldered jump ring.

3 String 2 Swarovski crystal pearls, 1/4" of French wire, and the soldered jump ring, leaving a 2" tail thread. Pass back through 1 pearl and tie an overhand knot. Pass back through the second pearl, and trim the tail thread. Place a small dot of Hypo-cement on the knot.

4 Use the clasp end of the thread to form an overhand knot. Place the Tri-Cord Knotter or awl into the knot before pulling tight. Use the tool to gently move the knot so that it is tight against the pearl and, when snug, pull tight.

5 String the remaining Swarovski crystal pearls and keep them 8–10" from the previous knot. Repeat Step 4 until 2 pearls remain.

6 Slide remaining pearls down to the previous knot. String ¼" of French wire and the other half of the clasp. Pass back through the last pearl. Tie a half hitch knot between the last 2 beads and pull tight. Pass back through the second-to-last pearl and trim thread. Place a small dot of Hypo-cement on the final knot.

Bracelet

Repeat Steps 1–6 to make a knotted pearl bracelet, attaching the silk/French wire directly to both sides of the clasp and substituting freshwater pearls for Swarovski crystal pearls.

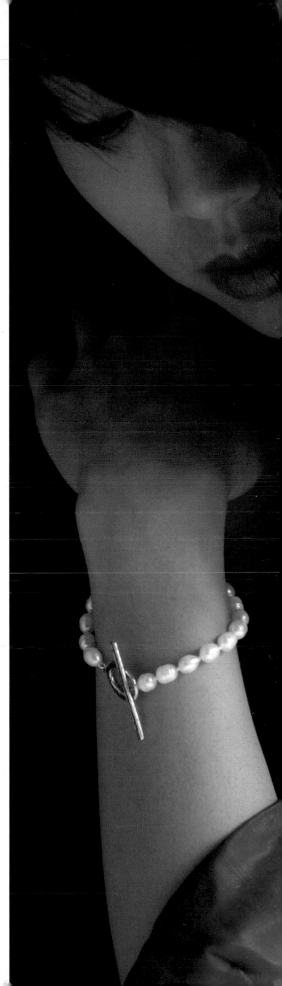

Purple Pearls

For the style of classic pearl knotting without the intricate handwork, string Delica beads in a matching or complementary color between each pair of pearls. In this piece, the small, uniform seed beads are a subtle contrast to the sparkling crystals, which create an elegant accent.

MATERIALS

68 burgundy Delicas

10 light amethyst 8mm Swarovski crystal rounds

6 light amethyst 8mm Swarovski rhinestone rounds

50 burgundy 10mm Swarovski crystal pearls

1 sterling silver 2mm crimp tube

1 sterling silver 3mm crimp cover

30" of .019 beading wire

TOOLS

Wire cutters

Crimping pliers

Bead stop

FINISHED SIZE

28" (71 cm)

1 Place a bead stop on one end of the wire. String 1 cylinder bead and 1 pearl thirty-three times.

2 String 1 cylinder bead, 1 crystal round, 1 cylinder bead, 1 pearl, 1 cylinder bead, 1 rhinestone round, 1 cylinder bead, 1 pearl, 1 cylinder bead, 1 crystal round, 1 cylinder bead, 1 pearl, 1 cylinder bead, 1 crystal round, 1 cylinder bead, 1 pearl, 1 cylinder bead, 1 rhinestone round, 1 cylinder bead, and 1 pearl, three times.

3 String 1 cylinder bead, 1 crystal round, 1 cylinder bead, 1 pearl, 1 cylinder bead, and 1 crimp tube.

4 Remove the bead stop and pass the wire through the crimp tube. Pull both ends of wire to snug the beads, and crimp the tube. Cover the crimp tube with the crimp cover.

Dark Beauties

In this long Tahitian-like strand of beads, the look of classic pearl knotting is replicated with a new product that emulates the look of knots. Wear it as a single rope strand, or use a strand separator and double the strand for a distinctive matinee-length piece. Choose a separator to match the occasion, or wear it in front to give the appearance of a pendant.

1 Mix the pearls into a bead soup.

2 String 1 Bead Bumper and 1 pearl ninety-three times.

3 String 1 Bead Bumper and 2 crimp tubes. Pass the other end of the wire back through the crimp tubes. Snug beads and crimp both tubes.

4 To use the strand separator, find the approximate middle of the strand of beads and close the strand separator around the beads. This cuts the beads in half, making it look like a two-strand piece. Another option would be to wrap the beads twice around the neck, with one strand longer than the other, then use the strand separator to cinch the bottom of the longer strand, making it look like a pendant or lariat.

MATERIALS

23 black 10mm Swarovski crystal pearls
23 dark gray 10mm Swarovski crystal pearls
23 light gray 10mm Swarovski crystal pearls
24 Tahitian 10mm Swarovski crystal pearls
94 black Bead Bumpers
Sterling silver strand separator
2 sterling silver 2mm crimp tubes
51" of .019 beading wire

TOOLS

Wire cutters
Crimping pliers

FINISHED SIZE

49¹/₂" (125.5 cm)

Coin of the Realm

Using a simple coin pearl with a red pearl accent, these simple yet chic earrings look fabulous in any part of the world, no matter what the currency.

1 Use a head pin to string 1 champagne pearl, 1 spacer, and 1 red pearl.

2 Use flat-nose pliers to grip the head pin ⅛" from the top of the red pearl and bend 90°. Use round-nose pliers to form a simple loop, but do not cut the wire. Attach the simple loop to the ear wire. Form a double-wrapped loop by wrapping the wire toward the pearl and then wrapping back toward the ear wire. (For more information, see Wireworking, page 114.)

3 Repeat Steps 1 and 2 to make the second earring.

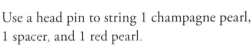

MATERIALS
2 dark red 4mm pearls
2 champagne 11mm coin pearls
2 Vermeil 2mm spacers
1 pair 14k gold ear wires
2 gold 14k head pins

TOOLS
Chain-nose pliers
Round-nose pliers
Wire cutters

FINISHED SIZE
1¼" (3.2 cm)

Mother-of-Pearl Radiance

Long considered less desirable than true pearls, mother-of-pearl is made of the same material—nacre—and can glow as beautifully as its much-prized cousin. In this simply strung piece, two colors of mother-of-pearl shine when paired with gold-filled rounds and a fun vermeil clasp.

1 Use a head pin to string 1 white mother-of-pearl. Form a wrapped loop. Repeat to make 44 white mother-of-pearl dangles and 22 brown mother-of-pearl dangles.

2 Use a crimp tube to attach 18" of wire to the first hole of one half of the clasp. String 2A, 1B, 1A, 1C, 1B, 1A, 1 white dangle, 1B, 1C, 1A, 1B, 1 brown dangle, 2A, 1 white dangle, 1A, 1 white dangle, 1B, 1C, 1A, 1 brown dangle, 1B, 1 white dangle, 1A, 1C, 1A, 1 white dangle, 1B, 1 brown dangle, 1A, 1 white dangle, 1A, 1 brown dangle, 1B, 1C, 1A, 1 brown dangle, 1B, 1 white dangle, 1A, 1C, 1B, 1 brown dangle, 2A, 1B, 1 white dangle, 1A, 1C, 1B, 1C, 1A, 2B, 1A, 1B, 1C, 1B, 1A, 1B, 1 crimp tube, and the first hole of the other half of the clasp. Pass back through the tube and crimp.

3 Use a crimp tube to attach 18" of wire to the second hole of one half of the clasp. String 1A, 1B, 1C, 1A, 3B, 1A, 1C, 1A, 1 brown dangle, 1B, 1A, 1 white dangle, 1A, 1 brown dangle, 1B, 1 white dangle, 1A, 1C, 1B, 1 white dangle, 1A, 1B, 1 white dangle, 1A, 1B, 1 white dangle, 1B, 1C, 1B, 1 brown dangle, 1A, 1 white dangle, 1B, 1C, 1B, 1 white dangle, 2B, 1 white dangle, 1A, 1B, 1A,

MATERIALS

134 white 6x10mm mother-of-pearl ovals (A)

125 brown 6x10mm mother-of-pearl ovals (B)

43 gold-filled 4mm spacers (C)

66 gold head pins

10 gold-filled 2mm crimp tubes

Vermeil five-strand hook-and-eye clasp

90" of gold .018 beading wire

TOOLS

Chain-nose pliers

Round-nose pliers

Wire cutters

Crimping pliers

FINISHED SIZE

18½" (47 cm)

1 brown dangle, 1B, 1C, 1A, 1B, 1 white dangle, 1B, 1C, 1B, 1 white dangle, 2B, 1A, 1C, 1B, 1A, 1B, 1A, 1 crimp tube, and the second hole of the other half of the clasp. Pass back through the tube and crimp.

4 Use a crimp tube to attach 18" of wire to the third hole of one half of the clasp. String 1B, 1C, 1A, 1B, 1A, 2B, 1C, 1A, 1B, 1 white dangle, 1B, 1 brown dangle, 1A, 1C, 1A, 1B, 1 white dangle, 1B, 1C, 1 A, 1B, 1 white dangle, 1B, 1 white dangle, 1A, 1 brown dangle, 1A, 1C, 1A, 1 white dangle, 1B, 1 brown dangle, 1A, 1B, 1 white dangle, 1B, 1 white dangle, 1B, 1C, 1B, 1 white dangle, 1B, 1A, 1C, 2B, 1A, 1B, 1 brown dangle, 1A, 1B, 1C, 1B, 1A, 1C, 1A, 1 crimp tube, and the third hole of the other half of the clasp. Pass back through the tube and crimp.

5 Use a crimp tube to attach 18" of wire to the fourth hole of one half of the clasp. String 1A, 1B, 1C, 1B, 1A, 1 white dangle, 1B, 1C, 1A, 1 brown dangle, 1B, 1A, 1 white dangle, 1B, 1A, 1C, 1B, 1 white dangle, 1A, 1B, 1 white dangle, 1A, 1 brown dangle, 1A, 1 white dangle, 1B, 1C, 1A, 1 brown dangle, 1A, 1 brown dangle, 1A, 1B, 1 white dangle, 1A, 1B, 1C, 1B, 1 white dangle, 1B, 1A, 1C, 1B, 1A, 1 white dangle, 1B, 1A, 1B, 1A, 1B, 1C, 1A, 1 crimp tube, and the fourth hole of the other half of the clasp. Pass back through the tube and crimp.

6 Use a crimp tube to attach 18" of wire to the fifth hole of one half of the clasp. String 1B, 1A, 2B, 1C, 1A, 2B, 1 white dangle, 1A, 1C, 1B, 1 brown dangle, 1B, 1A, 1B, 1 white dangle, 1B, 1C, 1B, 1 white dangle, 1A, 1 B, 1 white dangle, 1B, 1A, 1 brown dangle, 1A, 1C, 1B, 1 white dangle, 1A, 1 brown dangle, 1A, 1B, 1 white dangle, 1B, 1C, 1A, 1 white dangle, 1B, 1A, 1 white dangle, 1B, 1C, 1B, 1A, 1 white dangle, 1B, 1A, 1C, 1A, 1B, 1A, 1C, 2A, 2B, 1 crimp tube, and the fifth hole of the other half of the clasp. Pass back through the tube and crimp.

TINY GEMS:
Ancient Greeks believed that pearls were dew from the moon that oysters collected at night as they opened themselves and floated on the surface of the seas.

did you know . . .

The "Pearlies" of London

In the 1880s, a London street sweeper named Henry Croft had a uniquely budget-conscious solution for keeping up with the pearl-wearing elite. He covered his suit entirely with mother-of-pearl buttons! This quickly became a fad among Croft's fellow street laborers, who soon covered their suits and dresses with pounds of pearl buttons sewn in decorative arrangements and motifs. Although the Pearlies' numbers have diminished over time, the society is still active and wears button finery for special occasions, such as Queen Elizabeth's Silver Jubilee.

A procession of Pearly Kings and Queens, Southwark, London. Courtesy of Mary Evans Picture Library Ltd., London.

The Midas Touch

A fresh take on the Edwardian dog collar, this delicate but distinctive necklace makes a statement. Blending tiny white pearls with Biwa pearls in striking colors, the gold accents in this traditional collar evoke royalty and wealth. Completing the piece is a clasp inlaid with a single Biwa pearl.

MATERIALS

334 white 2x3mm seed pearls

9 white 6x20–25mm Biwa pearls

6 gold 6x20–25mm Biwa pearls

5 sterling silver 5x20mm five-strand spacer bars

Sterling silver multistrand box clasp with Biwa pearl inlay

10 sterling silver 2mm crimp tubes

75" of .014 beading wire

TOOLS

Wire cutters

Crimping pliers

FINISHED SIZE

12½" (31.5 cm)

1 Attach 15" of wire to one half of the clasp using a crimp tube.

2 String 13 seed pearls, the first hole of 1 spacer, 1 seed pearl, 1 white Biwa pearl, 8 seed pearls, the first hole of the second spacer, 1 seed pearl, 1 gold Biwa pearl, 7 seed pearls, the first hole of the third spacer, 1 seed pearl, 1 white Biwa pearl, 9 seed pearls, the first hole of the fourth spacer, 1 seed pearl, 1 gold Biwa pearl, 6 seed pearls, the first hole of the fifth spacer, 1 seed pearl, 1 white Biwa pearl, 3 seed pearls, 1 crimp tube, and the other half of the clasp. Pass back through the tube and crimp.

3 Repeat Step 1. String 13 seed pearls, the second hole of the first spacer, 17 seed pearls, the second hole of the second spacer, 17 seed pearls, the second hole of the third spacer, 17 seed pearls, the second hole of the fourth spacer, 16 seed pearls, the second hole of the fifth spacer, 11 seed pearls, 1 crimp tube, and the other half of the clasp. Pass back through the tube and crimp.

4 Repeat Step 1. String 4 seed pearls, 1 white Biwa pearl, 1 seed pearl, the third hole of the first spacer, 8 seed pearls, 1 gold Biwa pearl, the third hole of the second spacer, 8 seed pearls, 1 white Biwa pearl, 1 seed pearl, the third hole of the third spacer, 8 seed pearls, 1 gold Biwa pearl, 1 seed pearl, the third hole of the fourth spacer, 8 seed pearls, 1 white Biwa pearl, 1 seed pearl, the third hole of the fifth spacer, 11 seed pearls, 1 crimp tube, and the other half of the clasp. Pass back through the tube and crimp.

5 Repeat Step 1. String 12 seed pearls, the fourth hole of the first spacer, 17 seed pearls, the fourth hole of the second spacer, 16 seed pearls, the fourth hole of the third spacer, 17 seed pearls, the fourth hole of the fourth spacer, 16 seed pearls, the fourth hole of the fifth spacer, 11 seed pearls, 1 crimp tube, and the other half of the clasp. Pass back through the tube and crimp.

6 Repeat Step 1. String 12 seed pearls, the fifth hole of the first spacer, 1 seed pearl, 1 gold Biwa pearl, 8 seed pearls, the fifth hole of the second spacer, 1 seed pearl, 1 white Biwa pearl, 8 seed pearls, the fifth hole of the third spacer, 1 seed pearl, 1 gold Biwa pearl, 8 seed pearls, the fifth hold of the fourth spacer, 1 seed pearl, 1 white Biwa pearl, 8 seed pearls, the fifth hole of the fifth spacer, 1 seed pearl, 1 white Biwa pearl, 3 seed pearls, 1 crimp tube, and the other half of the clasp. Pass back through the tube and crimp.

TINY GEMS:
One of the oldest known pearl necklaces is in the Louvre Museum in Paris. It dates to the seventh century B.C. and is believed to be the prayer beads of a Persian princess.

Ladies in Dog Collars

Many of the most elegant ladies of the Gilded Age wore multi-strand pearl dog collars. Held in position by vertical spacers, the collar's strands of pearls often stretched a society woman's neck to its very limits. Even royals such as Queen Alexandra (right), wife of England's Edward VII, wore her pearl dog collar in official photos like the one at right.

Alexander Bassano, National Portrait Gallery, London

Cuff Deluxe

Burgundy seed beads form the base of this cuff and bring out the spectrum of glorious colors in these side-drilled coin pearls. Combining the two very different shapes in right-angle weave creates a sculptural and unexpected bracelet.

MATERIALS

168 burgundy size 0° seed beads
81 champagne 10mm side-drilled coin
  pearls
Sterling silver multistrand slide clasp
Burgundy Nymo size D beading thread

TOOLS

Scissors
Size 12 beading needle
Thread Heaven thread conditioner

FINISHED SIZE

7" (18 cm)

1 Use 8' of conditioned thread to string a tension bead leaving a 12" tail.

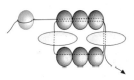

Figure 1

Unit 1: String 3 seed beads, 1 pearl, 3 seed beads, and 1 pearl. Pass through the first 3 seed beads and 1 pearl again (Figure 1).

Unit 2: String 3 seed beads, 1 pearl, and 3 seed beads. Pass through the pearl from the first unit and the first 3 seed beads strung in this unit (Figure 2).

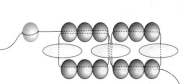

Figure 2

Unit 3: String 1 pearl, 3 seed beads, and 1 pearl. Pass through the 3 seed beads from the previous unit and all beads just strung (Figure 3).

Unit 4: Pass through the second set of seed beads strung in Unit 1. String 1 pearl and 3 seed

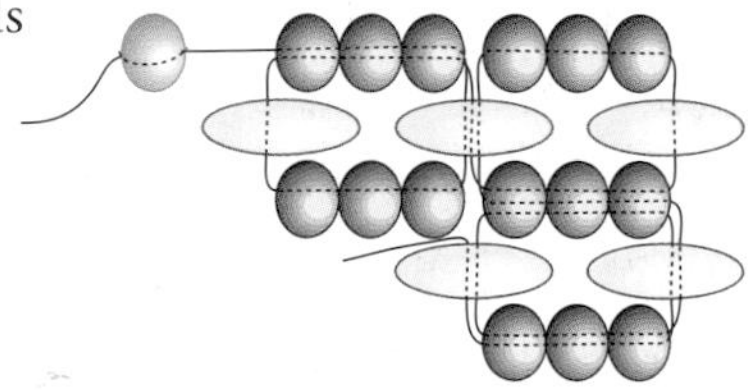

Figure 3

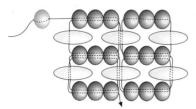

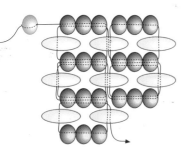

Figure 4

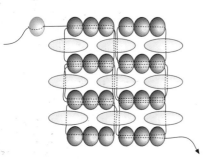

Figure 5

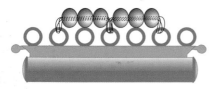

Figure 6

beads. Pass through the pearl from the previous unit, the seed beads from Unit 1, and the beads just strung (Figure 4).

Unit 5: String 1 pearl, 3 seed beads, and 1 pearl. Pass through the 3 seed beads from the previous unit and the first pearl strung in this unit (Figure 5).

Unit 6: String 3 seed beads and 1 pearl. Pass through the seed beads in Unit 3, the pearl from Unit 5, and the seed beads just strung (Figure 6).

2 Repeat Units 3–6 for a total of 27 rows.

3 String 1 hole of the clasp and pass back through 3 seed beads. Pass through another hole of the clasp and pass through the seed beads. Repeat several times. Repeat for the other 3 seed beads in the final row of the bracelet (Figure 7).

4 Remove the tension bead from the tail thread. Thread a needle and use the tail thread to repeat Step 3 to attach the bracelet to the other half of the clasp.

Figure 7

Back side of bracelet

Freshwater versus Sea Pearls

Pearl-bearing mollusks are found in rivers, lakes, bays, and oceans around the world. Freshwater pearls, which are produced by pearl mussels, are not as highly valued as saltwater pearls, primarily because they are usually smaller and not as perfectly round. However, they are more completely composed of nacre (source of the pearl's luster) than are their ocean-going cousins. This is because most are implanted only with a small piece of mantle tissue, around which nacre forms, making them almost pure nacre. Sea pearls, on the other hand, are seeded in pearl oysters with both a piece of tissue and a small spherical bead (usually mother-of-pearl). In smaller pearl oysters, such as the Akoya (*Pinctada fucata*), the layers of nacre that form around the bead can be somewhat thin, depending on how long the oyster remains in the water before harvest—anywhere from one to three years. The larger pearl oysters, *Pinctada maxima* and *Pinctada margaritifera,* which are found in the South Sea (Australia, Myanmar, Indonesia), produce much bigger pearls, with more layers of nacre than its saltwater competitor, the Akoya found in Japan and China. For those who want to add pearly accents to as many pieces of beadwork as possible, freshwater pearls are the answer to our dreams.

Cultured Pearls—Are They Real?

It may matter to a collector whether pearls are natural (formed without human intervention) or cultured (created by implanting a seed). For most of us, cultured pearls are the only pearls we will ever buy. And they are as real as any natural pearl, formed of precisely the same substance—nacre—and in the same natural process within the creature.

Natural pearls are mostly a phenomenon of the past, when pearl divers around the world risked their lives going to great depths to harvest pearl oysters and mussels. Because of their rarity and the extremes it took to collect them, natural pearls were the exclusive province of the royal and the wealthy until the early twentieth century. These days, natural pearls are mostly found in pre-1930s estate jewelry.

Even with carefully cultivated or cultured pearl oysters, about half of the mollusks do not survive; only 20 percent produce viable pearls; and of these only a small percentage (less than 5 percent) form fine-quality pearls.

Lucky for us, today's global periculture business (the culturing of pearls) has made it possible for almost anyone to own pearls. Even luckier, those of us who love to design and make our own jewelry can find affordable pearls in myriad shapes and colors.

special occasion

The best man has just toasted the bride and groom. Friends and family tap crystal champagne flutes, and the tinkling sound of joyful tribute fills the room. Tables are dressed with delicate soft pink silk streamers, and a sprinkling of golden rose petals tops ivory damask tablecloths. The wedding celebration feels intimate, full of personal, handcrafted decorative touches. Even your place card is handwritten by the bride.

Whether you're at a wedding, a graduation, or an intimate Valentine's dinner, you dress to add beauty and meaning to the occasion. In your finest attire, from warm velvet to sleek silk to delicate lace, the special touch of pearl jewelry makes you look and feel regal.

The luxurious look and feel of pearls are perfectly suited to special occasions. The joy of a champagne tribute is echoed in a necklace formed of diaphanous ribbons in colors from ivory to peach to lavender and almost-wine, embellished with soft pearls and silver wire accents. For a more glamorous approach, wear a striking lariat of black pearls and silver loops with a chandelier-like dangle. Or add drama to a strand of peach pearls with veined turquoise ovals, silver beads, and a pendant that evokes a shrine. Celebrate memorable times in unforgettable pearl jewelry that you've made yourself.

Champagne Necklace

Scattered pearls, wrapped with wire to sparkling ribbon, appear to bubble up like champagne in a glass flute. With six tiers of festive streamers, glints of silver, and subtly colored pearls, this bib-style necklace lends a festive air to any occasion.

MATERIALS

45 assorted white, gray, mauve, peach, and lavender 6x8mm pearls

2 sterling silver 20x25mm cones

Sterling silver 14mm box clasp with pearl inlay

156" of ³/₄" wide nylon ribbon

135" of 24-gauge sterling silver wire

8" of 22-gauge sterling silver wire

Craft glue

TOOLS

Tape measure

Scissors

Wire cutters

Chain-nose pliers

Round-nose pliers

Crimping pliers

FINISHED SIZE

19¹/₄" (49 cm) (shortest strand)

1 Cut the ribbon into six pieces, one each of the following lengths: 21", 23", 25", 27", 29", and 31."

2 Use 4" of 22-gauge wire to form a wrapped loop using the widest part of the round-nose pliers. Repeat to make a second loop.

3 Pass one end of the shortest ribbon through one of the loops. Use the end of this ribbon and the end of the next shortest ribbon to tie an overhand knot. Repeat with the other loop and the other ends of the ribbons.

4 Repeat Step 3 with the two middle lengths of ribbon, then the two longest lengths.

5 Place a drop of craft glue on each knot and let dry.

6 Use one wrapped loop wire to string 1 cone, making sure to conceal the knots in the cone. Form a wrapped loop that attaches to one half of the clasp. Repeat for the other half of the necklace.

7 Use 3" of 24-gauge wire to string 1 pearl. Center the pearl on the wire and bend both ends up 90°. Use your nondominant hand to hold the pearl and a section of the shortest ribbon together. Use your dominant hand to wrap one end of the wire around the ribbon as tightly as possible to secure the pearl in place. Repeat to wrap the other end of wire.

8 Repeat Step 7 to add a total of six pearls each to the three shortest strands of ribbon, eight pearls each to the next two longest strands, and nine pearls to the longest strand.

TINY GEMS:

Margarite is the archaic word for pearl, derived from the Latin word "margarita." It is also the likely origin of the name Margaret.

The Fine Art of Imitation

As far back as the Roman Empire, imitation pearls have graced beautiful jewelry. Even Elizabeth I of England, whose passion for pearls was well-known, mixed imitation pearls among the thousands of natural pearls that embellished her elaborate gowns. There were many recipes for imitation pearls through the centuries, some of them calling for ground-up seed pearls as an ingredient. Renaissance artist Leonardo da Vinci (1452–1519) concocted his own special recipe for imitation pearls. In his, small natural pearls were dissolved in lemon juice, the resulting paste dried into a powder, and the powder mixed with a beaten egg white to reconstitute it into a paste from which simulated pearls could be formed.

The best-known of the imitators, however, was a seventeenth-century French rosary maker named Jacquin, whose formula combined ground iridescent fish scales with lacquer. The resulting substance, called *essence d'orient*, was then placed inside small hollow glass beads, with wax added for weight. A variation on the rosary maker's formula and process is still used today; solid glass, mother-of-pearl, or plastic beads are alternately dipped into *essence d'orient* and allowed to dry.

Imitation pearls were a boon to costume jewelry designers of the early twentieth century. Famed American jewelry designer Miriam Haskell mixed real seed pearls with her trademark imitation baroque pearls to create luxurious, affordable jewelry. To ensure a supply of high-quality imitation pearls, Haskell commissioned skilled Czechoslovakian glass craftspeople to make her pearls. French fashion designer Gabrielle ("Coco") Chanel was among the first to accessorize haute couture clothing with imitation pearl jewelry. A great fan of pearls—she advocated wearing "ropes and ropes of pearls"—she was known to wear mixes of real and imitation pearls.

Even the most skillfully made imitation pearls can be distinguished from real pearls by the "tooth test." The texture of an imitation pearl's surface will be uniform, while a real pearl will have a natural unevenness. If you gently run the pearl along the edge of your teeth, a real pearl will have a somewhat gritty feel, while an imitation pearl will be smooth. If rubbing pearls against your teeth seems a little too visceral, simply rub two pearls together (again, gently). If you detect some resistance, they pass the "genuine" test. When shopping, also, be aware of some terms—faux, simulated, man-made, organic, "Mallorca," or fashion—which all indicate one thing: imitation pearls.

Sacred Vows Lariat

Two become one in this wedding necklace perfect for the bride. Double strands of pearls loop around a single strand connected with beautiful links. Shorter than a typical lariat, this asks to be worn close to the base of the throat—a princess-length piece to make her feel like royalty.

MATERIALS

7³/₄" (about 670) white 3–4mm button
  pearls
26 champagne 11mm coin pearls
2 sterling silver three-strand links
9 sterling silver 2mm crimp tubes
3 sterling silver 2" head pins
99" of .014 beading wire

TOOLS

Wire cutters
Crimping pliers
Chain-nose pliers
Round-nose pliers
Bead stop

FINISHED SIZE

21¹/₂" (54.5 cm)

1 Place a bead stop on the end of a 20" piece of wire. String 17½" (about 160) of button pearls. Remove the bead stop. Use both ends of wire to string 1 crimp tube and 1 loop of one link. Pass back through the tube and crimp. Repeat entire step twice, attaching a strand to the second loop of the link and a strand to the third loop of the link.

2 Use 13" of wire to string 1 crimp tube and the middle loop of one link. String 23 coin pearls, 1 crimp tube, and the middle loop of the other link. Pass back through the tube and crimp.

3 Use 13" of wire to string 1 crimp tube and an outside loop of the other side of the link. Pass back through the tube and crimp. String 10½" (about 95) of button pearls, 1 crimp tube, and an outside hole of the other link. Pass back through the tube and crimp. Repeat entire step for the other outside holes of the links.

4 Use a head pin to string 1 coin pearl. Form a wrapped loop that attaches to one of the remaining loops of the link. Repeat for the other two remaining loops.

TINY GEMS:

A couple who marries on a Monday is propitiously marrying on the day of the pearl and a day of wealth.

did you know . . .

The "I Do" Gem

Although a diamond is the modern emblem of engagement, it took a backseat to pearls throughout the nineteenth century, a time when the pearl was the ring gem of choice. Even in earlier centuries, royals and nobles decked themselves in pearls for their nuptials, and were expected to wear the gem that symbolized purity and fidelity. The trend continued into the twentieth century and beyond, extending to women of all backgrounds. Pearl jewelry as well as pearl decoration on gowns, veils, tiaras, and more continue to be a hallmark of the formal wedding.

Lavender Bouquet

Inspired by new love, this delicate but versatile piece is filled with special details. Violet and blue pearls evoke the freshness of the first spring colors, while careful stitching on the silver links adds dimension and organic accents to this one- to two-strand creation.

MATERIALS

110 purple size 11° seed beads

63 dark blue 5mm pearls

75 lavender 4x8mm potato pearls

10 sterling silver three-strand links

Sterling silver three-strand flower clasp

2 sterling silver 2mm crimp tubes

10" of purple .018 beading wire

Purple Nymo size D beading thread

TOOLS

Wire cutters

Crimping pliers

Scissors

Thread Heaven thread conditioner

Size 12 beading needle

FINISHED SIZE

20" (51 cm) (shortest strand)

1 Use 2' of conditioned thread to string the A-loops of two links. Pass down through the B-loop of the first link and the C-loop of the second link (Figure 1). Repeat several times for strength. Pass through the A-loops of the first two links and a third link. Pass back through the B-loop of the second link and the C-loop of the third link. Repeat several times for strength. Continue adding links in this manner, connecting the B-loop of the fifth link to the C-loop of the first link to form a circle. Pass through all loops again to secure.

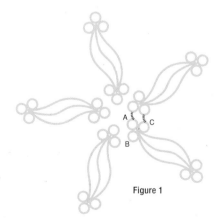

Figure 1

2 Pass up through a pair of B- and C-loops. String 1 lavender pearl and pass down through the opposite B- and C-loops (Figure 2). Repeat to secure.

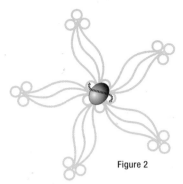

Figure 2

3 Pass up through the next B- and C-loop. String 4 seed beads and pass down through the next B- and C-loops. Repeat until you have a ring of seed beads around the pearl (Figure 3). Pass through all seed beads again.

4 String 2 seed beads, 1 dark blue pearl, and 2 seed beads. Skip 2 seed beads on the ring and pass through the next seed bead. Repeat for a total of 6 dark blue pearls around the lavender pearl (Figure 4). Weave through beads, tie knots to secure the thread, and trim.

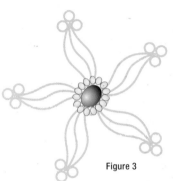

Figure 3

5 Attach the beading wire to 1 A-loop using a crimp tube (the A-loop at the opposite end of the link from the pearls just added). Cover the tube with a crimp cover. String 3 lavender, 1 seed bead, 1 dark blue, and 1 seed bead. String 5 lavender, 1 seed bead, 1 dark blue, 1 seed bead, 3 lavender, 1 seed bead, 1 dark blue, and 1 seed bead twice. String 3 lavender, 1 crimp tube, and the hook half of the clasp. Pass back through the tube. Crimp and cover.

6 Use a surgeon's knot to attach 10" of thread to one loop of the eye half of the clasp. String 3 lavender pearls, 1 seed bead, 1 dark blue pearl, 1 seed bead, 3 lavender pearls and the A-loop of 1 link. Pass back and forth through all beads a few times for strength. Tie and trim ends.

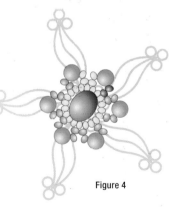

Figure 4

7 Repeat Step 6, substituting the following sequence of beads: Attach thread to the previous link and string 5 lavender pearls, 1 seed bead, 1 dark blue pearl, 1 seed bead, 3 lavender pearls, 1 seed bead, 1 dark blue pearl, 1 seed bead, 5 lavender pearls, and the A-loop of 1 link.

8 Repeat Step 6, attaching the strand to the previous link and the bottom right link of the flower.

9 Repeat Step 6, attaching 6" of thread to the other loop of the eye half of the clasp and stringing 5 lavender pearls between the clasp and link.

10 Use a surgeon's knot to attach 10" of thread to the previous link. String 3 lavender pearls, 1 seed bead, 1 dark blue pearl, 1 seed bead, 5 lavender pearls, 1 seed bead, 1 dark blue pearl, 1 seed bead, 3 lavender pearls, and the A-loop of 1 link. Pass back and forth through all beads a few times for strength. Tie and trim ends. Repeat entire step.

11 Use a surgeon's knot to attach 6" of thread to the previous link. String 3 lavender pearls and the A-loop of the bottom left link of the flower. Pass back and forth through all beads a few times for strength. Tie and trim ends.

Figure 5

12 Use a surgeon's knot to attach 8" of thread to the A-loop of a link. String 1 dark blue pearl and 1 seed bead. Pass back through the pearl and A-loop and up through the B-loop. String 1 dark blue pearl and 1 seed bead. Pass back through the pearl and B-loop and up through the C-loop. String 1 dark blue pearl and 1 seed bead. Pass back through the pearl and C-loop (Figure 5). Use both ends of thread to tie a knot and trim threads. Repeat entire step for both ends of all links, including the links in the flower focal piece.

Kokichi Mikimoto (1858–1954)
Father of the Cultured Pearl Industry

Although others before him had succeeded in culturing pearls—notable among them, the Swedish naturalist Carl von Linné or Linnaeus (1717–1778)— Kokichi Mikimoto, the son of a Japanese noodle shop owner, would launch the most successful cultivation and promotion program for cultured pearls. Mikimoto, who bought the patents for culturing Akoya pearls from his rivals marine biologist Dr. Tokichi Nishikawa and carpenter Tatsuhei Mise, was an ambitious marketeer. Despite resistance to the introduction of cultured pearls into the marketplace at the turn of the twentieth century, when the pearls were somewhat unimpressive in their size and quality, Mikimoto was a tireless innovator and promoter of the cultured pearl. After years of trial-and-error experimentation, these cultivated pearls gained ground beginning in the 1920s.

In nature, a perfectly round pearl is a rare thing, as are matched beauties on a strand. Mikimoto developed techniques to produce pearls of uniform roundness. His enterprise also developed bleaching and coloring techniques to ensure uniform color and eliminate small blemishes on the pearl's surface. Although the Japanese pearl industry was relatively inactive during World War II, when the government considered it inessential, it sprang into action once more during the Allied Forces Occupation. Tens of thousands of U.S. servicemen returned to the states with strands of Mikimoto pearls for their sweethearts and relatives. The souvenirs were a great success, and cultivated pearls have kept jewelry lovers in lustrous strands ever since.

Pearl Fusion

The combination of peach pearls and turquoise nuggets begins in a handcrafted pendant and continues throughout this multistrand necklace. With a sterling silver clasp and Thai silver bead accents, this simple but striking piece blends materials and cultures for a showstopping effect.

1 Cut the wire in half. Use both wires to string 1 crimp tube and the bar half of the clasp. Pass back through the tube and crimp. Use both wires to string one end of the chain.

2 Use one wire to string 6 cornerless cubes. String 1 turquoise, 1 cornerless cube, 1 seed bead, and 1 cornerless cube fourteen times. String 1 turquoise and 1 cornerless cube. Place a bead stop on the end of this wire and set aside.

3 Use the other wire to string 6 cornerless cubes. String 3 pearls and 1 cornerless cube nineteen times. Place a bead stop on the end of this wire and set aside.

MATERIALS

14 size 8° seed beads

57 peach 6–8mm pearls

15 turquoise 20–25mm graduated ovals

35x75mm ceramic and pearl pendant with Thai silver charm

59 Thai silver 2mm cornerless cubes

40mm sterling silver toggle clasp

2 sterling silver 2x3mm crimp tubes

17¼" of 3mm sterling silver chain

40" of .019 beading wire

TOOLS

Wire cutters

Crimping pliers

Bead stops

FINISHED SIZE

17½" (43 cm) (shortest strand)

4 Use the chain to string the pendant.

5 Remove bead stops. Use both wires to string the other end of the chain, 1 crimp tube, and the ring half of the clasp. Pass back through the tube and crimp.

TINY GEMS:

During the Renaissance, the privileged classes often depended upon the pearls they wore to illuminate them in dark interiors of castles lit only by candles.

Buddha and the Cultural Revolution

From as early as the fifth century B.C., the Chinese cultivated freshwater pearls in rivers and streams. In addition to half-spheres or other forms, Buddha-shaped small metal castings were placed between the shell and the mantle of freshwater pearl mussels. Nacre formed around the shapes, creating what are known as "blister pearls." To harvest the pearl Buddhas, they were cut away from the shell against which they had formed. For the tourist trade and for religious purposes, these pearl Buddhas are still cultivated in China today. Even figures such as Chairman Mao have been celebrated in the form of a pearl.

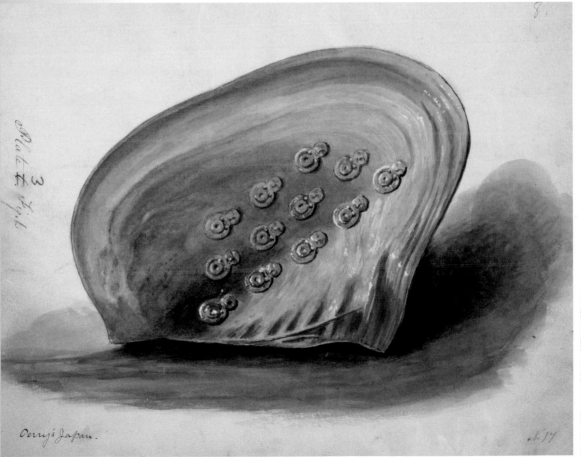

Copper Romance

MATERIALS

58 copper 3mm Swarovski crystal pearls (A)

59 bronze 3mm Swarovski crystal pearls (B)

59 powder almond 3mm Swarovski crystal pearls (C)

50 Tahitian 5mm Swarovski crystal pearls (D)

25 copper 6mm Swarovski crystal pearls (E)

30 bronze 6mm Swarovski crystal pearls (F)

25 powder almond 6mm Swarovski crystal pearls (G)

25 copper 8mm Swarovski crystal pearls (H)

25 bronze 8mm Swarovski crystal pearls (I)

25 powder almond 8mm Swarovski crystal pearls (J)

21 copper 10mm Swarovski crystal pearls (K)

20 bronze 10mm Swarovski crystal pearls (L)

21 powder almond 10mm Swarovski crystal pearls (M)

Sterling silver seven-strand Gucci-style clasp

8 sterling silver 2mm crimp tubes

80" of .019 beading wire

Dark blue Nymo size D beading thread

Beige Nymo size D beading thread

TOOLS

Scissors

Thread Heaven thread conditioner

Size 12 beading needles

Wire cutters

Crimping pliers

FINISHED SIZE

16¼" (41.5 cm) (shortest strand)

Large pearls and small beaded rings in hues of copper, bronze, and almond are embellished with dashes of dark Tahitian blue. The four strands of this choker recall the tumbling of blue waves onto a rocky shore. Truly, a fine romance.

1 Use 6" of dark blue conditioned thread to string 5D. Pass through the pearls again to form a loop and knot. Pass through the pearls again, knot, and trim ends. Repeat for a total of 10 D-rings. Repeat, using beige thread, to make 5 E-rings, 6 F-rings, and 5 G-rings. Repeat, using 7 pearls, to make 8 A-rings, 8 B-rings, and 8 C-rings.

2 Attach 20" of beading wire to one half of the clasp using a crimp tube.

3 String 1C, *1J, 1H, 1 B-ring, 1J, 1H, 1I, 1 C-ring, 1H, 1I, 1J, 1J, 1H, 1 D-ring, 1I, 1J, 1 A-ring, 1I, 1J, 1H, 1 D-ring, 1I, 1J, 1 A-ring, 1I, 1B-ring, 1H, 1 C-ring, 1J*, 1H, 1 D-ring, and 1I. Repeat from * to *. String 1I, 1B, 1 crimp tube, and the other half of the clasp. Pass back through the tube and crimp.

4 Repeat Step 2. String 1C, 1M, 1 E-ring, 1L, 1M, 1K, 1 F-ring, 1M, 1K, 1L, 1 G-ring, 1K, 1L, 1M, 1 E-ring, 1L, 1M, 1K, 1 F-ring, 1M, 1K, 1L, 1 D-ring, 1M, 1K, 1L, 1 G-ring, 1K, 1L, 1M, 1 E-ring, 1L, 1M, 1K, 1 F-ring, 1M, 1K, 1L, 1 D-ring, 1M, 1K, 1L, 1B, 1 crimp tube, and the other half of the clasp. Pass back through the tube and crimp.

did you know . . .

Still a Fashion Favorite

Few of us, no matter our age, have not seen photo stills from *Breakfast at Tiffany's*, in which Audrey Hepburn (as Holly Golightly) stands outside Tiffany's in a black evening dress looking through the windows of the exclusive New York jewelry store. Hair swept in a fashionable up-do, Hepburn wears an impressive piece of pearl costume jewelry around her neck, multiple strands of large imitation pearls that symbolize the wealth and glamour to which Holly aspires. That iconic image seems to say it all: Pearls make the woman. Despite fashion's fluctuations, pearls are a permanent part of the style pantheon for women of all walks of life. Such legendary figures as Coco Chanel, Princess Grace Kelly, Jacqueline Kennedy Onassis, and Princess Diana were routinely seen in public and photographed in both classic pearl jewelry—the single or double princess-length strand—as well as dramatic layers of pearl ropes, jeweled pearl chokers, and pearl-embellished special-occasion clothing. Each fall season, as runway shows present haute couture fashions, pearls are used in the collections of many designers. Whether as accessories or as extravagant embellishment on gowns, the gem carries the message of continuity, as well as "cool." Pearls are a legacy gem, passed down through the generations. They are the serene sisters of bling, glowing from within to light up a woman's face rather stealing the show for themselves.

Midnight Tassel

A dangling handstitched tassel of seed beads
and black pearls punctuates this spectacular
necklace, which alternates oval and top-drilled
pearls separated by sophisticated wavy jump
rings. The Y shape and black baroque pearls
create a treasure with a touch of whimsy
and more than a hint of drama.

MATERIALS

30 silver size 11° seed beads

100 black size 11° seed beads

26 black 8x12mm pearls

31 black 8x12 top-drilled pearls

6 sterling silver 16mm soldered wavy
    jump rings

Sterling silver lock clasp

12 sterling silver 2mm crimp tubes

12 sterling silver crimp covers

33" of .019 beading wire

6" of sterling silver 22-gauge wire

Black Nymo size D beading thread

TOOLS

Wire cutters

Crimping pliers

Flat-nose pliers

Round-nose pliers

FINISHED SIZE

22" (56 cm)

1 Use 4' of conditioned thread to string a tension bead,
leaving a 6" tail. String 1 pearl, 5 black seed beads,
1 pearl, 5 black seed beads, 1 pearl, and 5 black seed
beads. Pass back through the first pearl strung. String
5 black seed beads and pass back through the second pearl
strung. String 5 black seed beads and pass back through the
third pearl strung. String 5 black seed beads (Figure 1).
Pass through all beads again, pulling tight to form a tube.
Tie a square knot using the tail and working threads.

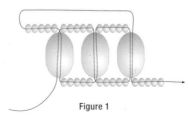

Figure 1

Figure 2

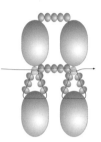

Figure 3

2 Pass through 3 black seed beads. *String 1 pearl and 1 silver seed bead. Pass back through the pearl (Figure 2). Pass through 5 black seed beads. Repeat once from *. String 1 pearl and 1 silver seed bead. Pass back through the pearl. Pass through all black seed beads again and pass back down through 1 pearl and 1 silver seed bead.

3 String 7 black seed beads and pass through the next silver seed bead. Repeat twice. *Pass through 1 black seed bead. String 1 silver seed bead. Skip 1 black seed bead and pass through the next black seed bead. Repeat twice. Pass through the next silver seed bead. Repeat from * twice.

4 String 3 black seed beads, 1 top-drilled pearl, and 3 black seed beads. Pass through the silver again to form a loop (Figure 3). Pass through 3 black seed beads. Repeat entire step to form 6 loops around the base of the tassel.

5 Use 6" of 22-gauge wire and 1 top-drilled pearl to form a wrapped loop bail. String 25 black seed beads. Pass the wire through the center of the tassel. String 1 pearl and form a wrapped loop that attaches to 1 jump ring.

6 Attach 6" of beading wire to the jump ring used in Step 5 using a crimp tube. Cover the tube with a crimp cover. String 6 pearls, a second jump ring (the jump ring should be large enough to slide over the pearls), 1 crimp tube, and a third jump ring. Pass back through the tube; crimp and cover.

7 Attach 6" of beading wire to the third jump ring using a crimp tube. Cover the tube with a crimp cover. String 12 top-drilled pearls, 1 crimp tube, and a fourth jump ring. Pass back through the tube; crimp and cover.

8 Attach 6" of beading wire to the fourth jump ring using a crimp tube. Cover the tube with a crimp cover. String 6 pearls, 1 crimp tube, and one half of the clasp. Pass back through the tube; crimp and cover.

9 Attach 3" of beading wire to the other half of the clasp using a crimp tube. Cover the tube with a crimp cover. String 1 pearl, 1 crimp tube, and a fifth jump ring. Pass back through the tube; crimp and cover.

10 Attach 6" of beading wire to the fifth jump ring using a crimp tube. Cover the tube with a crimp cover. String 6 pearls, 1 crimp tube, and a sixth jump ring. Pass back through the tube; crimp and cover.

11 Attach 6" of beading wire to the sixth jump ring using a crimp tube. Cover the tube with a crimp cover. String 12 top-drilled pearls, 1 crimp tube, and the second jump ring. Pass back through the tube; crimp and cover.

did you know . . .

La Peregrina, or "The Incomparable"

At the beginning of the sixteenth century, an exquisite pear-shaped white pearl was fished from the waters of the Americas (most likely the Gulf of Panama or off the coast of Venezuela). The enormous treasure, about 10 grams in weight, was presented by Spanish conquistador Balboa to King Ferdinand V. Over the centuries, the legendary pearl has passed through many royal hands, including those of Mary Tudor, Queen Margarita of Spain, Joseph Bonaparte of Spain, and Prince Louis Napoleon of France. The pearl's current owner is actress Elizabeth Taylor. In 1969, Ms. Taylor's husband Richard Burton purchased the pearl at auction as a Valentine's Day gift for her. After the pearl was personally delivered to her at her Las Vegas hotel room, Ms. Taylor lost the pearl in a plush carpet. Lucky for her and for the pearl, her pet dog held the pearl in his mouth—and had not yet swallowed the beauty when it was discovered.

Cleopatra's Pricey Wager

According to the writings of Roman scholar Pliny the Elder (23–79 B.C.), Egyptian queen Cleopatra bet Roman general Mark Anthony that she could serve him the most expensive meal ever made. She is said to have won the wager by dissolving one of her large pearl earrings in a cup of wine and drinking it. While this makes for a legendary tale, it's unlikely that Cleopatra could have so easily dissolved a huge fine pearl in a glass of wine without first crushing it. But the story as told is unforgettable.

The Birth of Venus, Sandro Botticelli, circa 1485, Uffizi Gallery, Florence, Italy.

Ancient Rome—Loving Pearls to Excess

In excavations and ancient art found throughout the Roman Empire, pearls play a starring role. Fashionable women of high standing wore earrings, hair ornaments, necklaces, bracelets, rings, and more, but their pearls were not merely objects of adornment. They also represented the power of an elite class, and they were material wealth. In Roman mythology, pearls were dedicated to Venus, the goddess of love and beauty, whose own pearl-like emergence from a shell in the sea links her to the gem. The nobility's hunger for pearl display went so far as to cause them to decorate shoes and feet, the fabric of couches, and, in the case of the Emperor Caligula, even a horse. Julius Caesar once bought a single pearl for 6 million sesterces (about $7.5 million U.S. today), which he gave to his mistress, the mother of Brutus. Historian Suetonius noted that this extravagant pearl gift represented "the spoils of nations in an ear." He also wrote that one of the reasons Caesar invaded Britain in 55 B.C. was to acquire pearls.

fashion-forward

When your best friend called to invite you to the gallery opening for an avant-garde metal sculptor's show, you said, "I can't wait!" Best of all, the gallery is in a chic city loft, with floor-to-ceiling windows that look out on the riverfront and its geometric skyline. You can already imagine the sounds of murmuring appreciation, laughter, excited greetings. Everyone will wear black for dramatic effect—and so will you.

In a setting filled with adventurous, artistic souls, creative handmade jewelry resonates with the spirit of the evening. This is your chance to express your individual style. Create a showstopping necklace by mixing bold metallic ingredients—shiny smooth and hammered oval silver chains—with black, white, and teal pearls to make a statement in contrasts: hard and soft, dark and light. For an evening with friends at a fashionable tapas bar, debut a rope of silvery braided fiber strands with a variety of simple pearl charms woven into the layers. Or maybe you want to flash a vibrant bracelet of stylish oval silver chain with dreamy green pearls wirewrapped to the links.

The fun of making pearl jewelry with an edge includes working with the more improbable colors of dyed pearls (from berry shades to bright iridescents), then partnering them with metals, polymer, seed beads, shell, fiber, and more. Give in to the impulse to bead pearl jewelry that blends romantic accents with urban chic. Then make your entrance in style!

Chain Reaction

Huge links of oval silver chain are divided by small classic white pearls, large sexy black pearls, and spunky teal pearls. The contrasting surface of the silver links, from hammered texture to mirror-smooth, reflects the evening's glow, and a hammered silver oval button toggle clasp brings this fresh look together.

MATERIALS

26 white 3x5mm pearls

65 teal 6mm pearls

15 black 8x12mm pearls

25mm sterling silver hammered button toggle clasp

4 sterling silver 2mm crimp tubes

4 sterling silver crimp covers

2 sterling silver 8mm jump rings

2 sterling silver 6mm jump rings

36" of sterling silver 24-gauge wire

20" of silver .018 beading wire

24" of sterling silver smooth oval chain

24" of sterling silver hammered oval chain

TOOLS

Wire cutters

Crimping pliers

Round-nose pliers

Chain-nose pliers

Flat-nose pliers

FINISHED SIZE

18" (45.5 cm)

1 Cut the hammered chain into one 1-link piece, two 2-link pieces, two 3-link pieces, three 4-link pieces, and one 5-link piece. Repeat with the smooth chain.

2 Use 3" of 24-gauge wire to form a wrapped loop that attaches to a 4-link piece of hammered chain. String 1 white pearl, 3 teal pearls, and 1 white pearl, and form a wrapped loop that attaches to a 1-link piece of smooth chain. Use 3" of 24-gauge wire to form a wrapped loop that attaches to the 1-link piece of chain. String 1 teal pearl, 1 black pearl, and 1 teal pearl, and form a wrapped loop that attaches to the 5-link piece of hammered chain. Use 3" of 24-gauge wire to form a wrapped loop that attaches to the other end of the 5-link piece of chain. String 1 white pearl, 3 teal pearls, and 1 white pearl and form a wrapped loop that attaches to a 4-link piece of smooth chain. Use 3" of 24-gauge wire to form a wrapped loop that attaches to the other end of the 4-link piece of chain. String 1 teal pearl, 1 black pearl, and 1 teal pearl, and form a wrapped loop that attaches to a 3-link piece of hammered chain. Set aside.

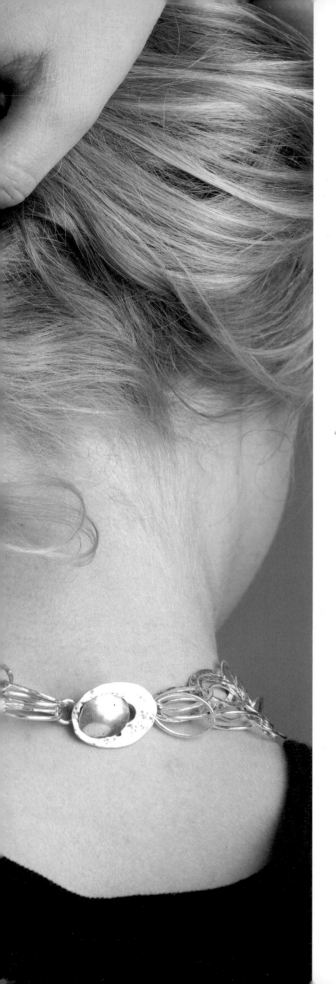

3 Use 3" of 24-gauge wire to form a wrapped loop that attaches to a 2-link piece of smooth chain. String 1 teal pearl, 1 black pearl, and 1 teal pearl and form a wrapped loop that attaches to a 1-link piece of hammered chain. Use 3" of 24-gauge wire to form a wrapped loop that attaches to the 1-link piece of chain. String 1 white pearl, 3 teal pearls, and 1 white pearl, and form a wrapped loop that attaches to a 4-link piece of smooth chain. Use a crimp tube to attach 10" of beading wire to the other end of the 4-link piece of chain. Cover the crimp tube with a crimp cover. String 1 teal pearl, 1 black pearl, 1 teal pearl, 1 white pearl, 3 teal pearls, and 1 white pearl three times. String 1 teal pearl, 1 black pearl, 1 teal pearl, 1 crimp tube, and a 4-link piece of hammered chain. Pass back through the tube; crimp and cover. Set aside.

4 Use 3" of 24-gauge wire to form a wrapped loop that attaches to a 3-link piece of smooth chain. String 1 white pearl, 3 teal pearls, and 1 white pearl and form a wrapped loop that attaches to a 4-link piece of hammered chain. Use a 3" piece of 24-gauge wire to form a wrapped loop that attaches to the other end of the 4-link chain. String 1 teal pearl, 1 black pearl, and 1 teal pearl, and form a wrapped loop that attaches to a 2-link piece of smooth chain. Use 3" of 24-gauge wire to form a wrapped loop that attaches to the other end of the 2-link chain. String 1 white pearl, 3 teal pearls, and 1 white pearl, and form a wrapped loop that attaches to a 3-link piece of hammered chain. Use 3" of 24-gauge wire to form a wrapped loop that attaches to the other end of the 3-link chain. String 1 teal pearl, 1 black pearl, and 1 teal pearl, and form a wrapped loop that attaches to a 5-link piece of smooth chain. Set aside.

5 Attach 10" beading wire to a 2-link piece of hammered chain using a crimp tube. Cover the tube with a crimp cover. String 1 white pearl, 3 teal pearls, 1 white pearl, 1 teal pearl, 1 black pearl, and 1 teal pearl three times. String 1 white pearl, 3 teal pearls, 1 white pearl, 1 crimp tube, and a 4-link piece of smooth chain. Pass back through the tube; crimp and cover. Use 3" of 24-gauge wire to form a wrapped loop that attaches to the other end of the 4-link chain. String 1 teal pearl, 1 black pearl, and 1 teal pearl, and form a wrapped loop that attaches to a 2-link piece of hammered chain. Use 3" of 24-gauge wire to form a wrapped loop that attaches to the other end of the 2-link chain. String 1 white pearl, 3 teal pearls, and 1 white pearl, and form a wrapped loop that attaches to a 3-link piece of smooth chain. Set aside.

6 Attach a 6mm jump ring to the button (bar) half of the toggle. Attach another 6mm jump ring to the 6mm jump ring.

7 Use an 8mm jump ring to attach all four strands to one half of the clasp. Repeat for the other half of the necklace.

TINY GEMS:

An ancient myth from India describes the offerings the elements made to the deity. Air offered a rainbow, fire a meteor, earth a ruby, and sea a pearl. The rainbow formed a halo about the head of the god, the meteor was a lamp, the ruby decorated the forehead of the god, and the pearl was worn upon the heart.

Global Pearls

Round beads, round shapes, round bracelet. Materials and colors fuse together flawlessly in this chunky treat for the wrist. Twelve seed beads hidden inside each polymer round help to fill the large hole and prevent the thread from showing between beads.

MATERIALS

79 metallic blue size 11° seed beads

31 gold 3x5mm oval pearls

31 copper 4x6mm button pearls

5 teal 10x12mm oval pearls

5 various 16–18mm polymer clay
   rounds

40" of black 6 lb FireLine beading thread

TOOLS

Scissors

Size 12 beading needle

Thread burner

FINISHED SIZE

9" (23 cm)

1 Slide the needle to the center of the thread. Use both ends of thread to tie a surgeon's knot.

2 String 1 copper, 12 seed beads, 1 polymer, 1 copper, and 1 teal five times. String 1 copper, 1 seed bead, and 11 gold. Pass back through the last seed bead and copper strung.

3 String 1 seed bead, 1 gold, 1 copper, 1 seed bead, 1 copper, 1 gold, and 1 seed bead. Skip the teal and pass back through the next copper, polymer (through the seed beads) and copper. Repeat entire step four times. Tie a surgeon's knot.

4 Pass back through 1 copper, 1 polymer (and seed beads) and 1 copper. *String 1 seed bead, 1 gold, 1 copper, 1 seed bead, 1 copper, 1 gold, and 1 seed bead. Skip the teal and pass back through the next copper, polymer (through the seed beads) and copper. Repeat from * three times. String 1 seed bead, 1 gold, 1 copper, 1 seed bead, 1 copper, 1 gold, and 1 seed bead. Pass through the copper, seed bead, and 11 gold to reinforce the loop. Pass back through all beads. Tie a surgeon's knot. Trim threads with a thread burner.

Columbus and "The Great Age of Pearls"

Before Columbus' exploration of the New World, pearls, which were valued more highly than gold, were supplied almost exclusively from the depths of the Indian Ocean. After gaining sponsorship from King Ferdinand and Queen Isabella of Spain in 1492, Columbus set sail with a royal wish list—and pearls were at the very top of it. He returned to Spain without the precious gems after his first voyage to the Caribbean (which he mistakenly named the West Indies). Finally, during his third voyage, he found pearls off the coast of Venezuela. Although he still didn't collect quantities of pearls, he did sail past the islands of Cubagua and Margarita, the area that would become known as the "Pearl Coast." Men who sailed with Columbus managed to pocket good supplies of Venezuelan pearls, which they promptly sold when they returned to Spain. Although Columbus himself never profited from the discovery of pearls in the New World, he opened the door to exploitation of these waters for the next 150 years. Pearls flooded the markets of Renaissance Europe, fueling an era of extravagance and rich artistic development. Seville, Spain, became the heart of the pearl market, while English, French, and Dutch pirates regularly raided Spanish ships for pearls.

The vast harvests of New World pearls created a demand bordering on obsession among European royalty for fabulous quantities of the gem to display in jewelry, embellished clothing, and *objets d'art*. By the late seventeenth century, however, the Venezuelan pearl fishery was depleted. From this time up until the early twentieth century, Sri Lanka and India returned to being the primary suppliers of pearls.

Catch of the Day

Pearl and silver charms are captured in this seven-foot-long "net" of braided cord, which is designed to wrap several times around the neck. Enjoy blending fiber and charms, then choose to wear the finished rope long and delicate or short and ornate.

1 Cut the cord into three 90" pieces. Divide the charms into two groups.

2 Use overhand knots to tie half of the charms to one piece of cord, spacing them evenly. Repeat with a second piece of cord and the remaining charms, making sure the charms on this cord are staggered between the charms on the first cord.

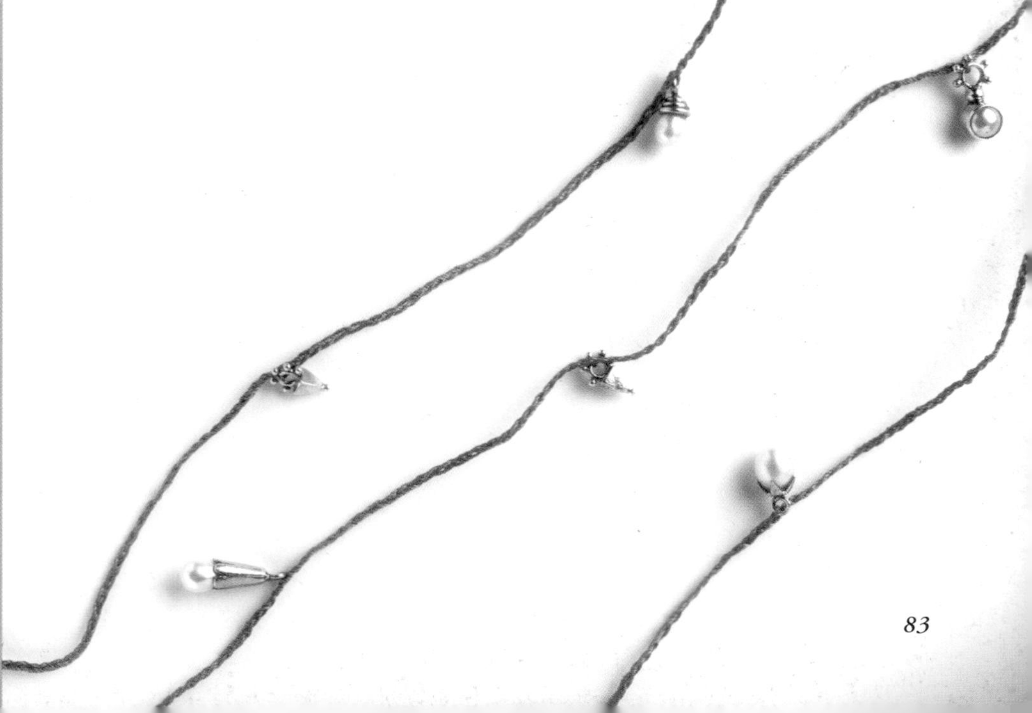

MATERIALS

8 sterling silver 6x10mm triangle charms

18 assorted sterling silver and pearl 6x10–8x20mm charms

Sterling silver box clasp with pearl inlay

2 sterling silver 3mm crimp tubes

270" of gray C-Lon Bead Cord

TOOLS

Scissors

Mighty Crimper crimping pliers

FINISHED SIZE

92" (234 cm)

3 Hold one end of each piece of cord together and use them to string 1 crimp tube and one half of the clasp. Pass back through the tube and crimp.

4 Braid the three cords together.

5 Repeat Step 3.

TINY GEMS:
According to Hindu legend, the god Krishna discovered the pearl when he fished it from the sea as a gift for his daughter on her wedding day.

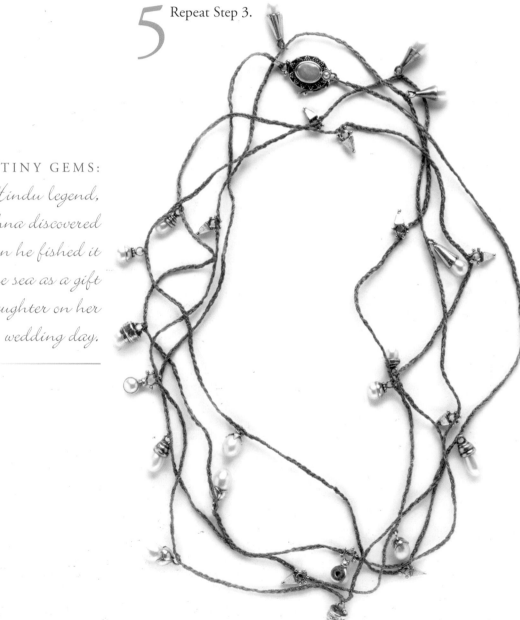

Off the Grid

Begin with a base of green and orange seed
beads stitched into a right-angle weave grid,
and embellish it with a scattering of dark green
pearls. Complete the cuff with a beaded triple
closure of loops and pearls for a finished piece
that's anything but square.

1 To begin the base, use 10' of conditioned thread
to string a tension bead, leaving a 12" tail.

2 Use single-needle right-angle weave to make a
bracelet base 29 units wide and 6 units tall, following
the directions below.

Row 1, Unit 1: String 3A, 2B, 3A, and 2B. Pass through
the first 3A and 2B again (Figure 1).

Row 1, Unit 2: String 3A, 2B, and 3A. Pass through the
2B from the previous and the first 3A and 2B from
this unit again (Figure 2).

Row 1, Units 3–29: Repeat Row 1, Unit 2. On Unit 29,
end by passing through only the first 3A of this
unit again.

Row 2, Unit 1: String 2B, 3A, and 2B. Pass through
the 3A from the final unit in the previous row and all
beads just strung (Figure 3).

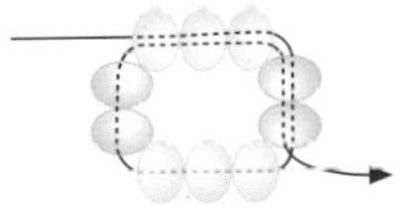

Figure 1

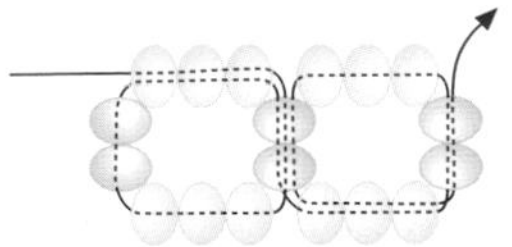

Figure 2

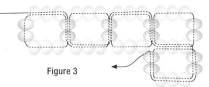

Figure 3

MATERIALS

5 g green/gold translucent size
  11° seed beads (A)

5 g orange white-lined size 11°
  seed beads (B)

5 g metallic green size 11° seed
  beads (C)

32 green 6mm pearls

Green Nymo size D beading thread

TOOLS

Scissors

Size 12 beading needle

Thread burner

FINISHED SIZE

6³/₄" (17 cm)

Row 2, Unit 2: Pass back through the 3A from the bottom of the unit in Row 1. String 2B and 3A. Pass through the 2B from the previous unit, back through the 3A from the previous row, and through the 2B just strung (Figure 4).

Row 2, Unit 3: String 3A and 2B. Pass through the 3A from the bottom of the unit in Row 1, the 2A from the previous unit, and the five beads just strung (Figure 5).

Row 2, Units 4–29: Repeat Row 2, Unit 2 and Row 2, Unit 3 to the end of the row.

Rows 3–6: Repeat Rows 1–2 twice.

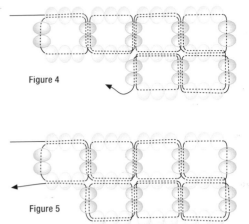

Figure 4

Figure 5

3 Begin embellishing the base. Weave through beads to exit from a group of 3A in the first column. String 1 pearl and pass through the 3A at the bottom of the same unit (Figure 6). Weave through beads to repeat in the next column, placing the bead in a different spot on the column. Repeat to stitch 1 pearl into each of the 29 columns.

Figure 6

4 Weave through beads to exit the final 3A strung. String 1C and pass through the next 3A. Repeat for the length of the bracelet. Repeat, adding 1A between each group of 2B on the edge of the bracelet. Repeat on the other two sides of the bracelet, adding 1C between each unit, omitting the corners.

5 To add a closure, weave through beads to exit the C between the first and second rows of the final column. String 16C (or as many C as needed to fit around a pearl). Pass back through the first C strung, then pass through the C of the final column again (Figure 7). Pass through all beads again to reinforce. Repeat to add a loop between the third and fourth rows and again between the fifth and sixth rows. Weave thread through beads and tie knots to secure. Trim thread.

Figure 7

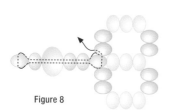

Figure 8

6 Remove the tension bead and place a needle on the tail thread. Weave through beads to exit the C between the first and second rows. String 2C, 1 pearl, and 2C. Skip the last C strung and pass back through 1C, the pearl, and 2C (Figure 8). Pass through all beads again to reinforce the closure. Repeat between the third and fourth rows and again between the fifth and sixth rows. Weave thread through beads and tie knots to secure. Trim thread.

TINY GEMS:
Because Russia had a vast supply of freshwater baroque pearls in its rivers, the gem was a favorite in both religious icons and jewelry. By the seventeenth century, every Russian woman had items of lacy pearl beadwork in her wardrobe.

did you know . . .

The Mississippi—Muddy and Full of Pearls

Pearl-bearing mussels in inland rivers and streams have long been the source of freshwater pearls throughout the world. Although people of the indigenous Hopewell culture collected massive amounts of pearls from the Mississippi and its tributaries until around A.D. 200, the river's pearls were not again heavily exploited until the mid-nineteenth century. By the 1880s, the boom was on, fishing first for pearls and later for pearl shells, the source of mother-of-pearl for buttons. Although the pearl fishery came close to being depleted, both fashion's move away from pearl buttons and conservation efforts may have saved it in time. Today, the Mississippi supplies most of the mother-of-pearl nuclei used in the cultured pearl industry.

Ocean Wonders

A reminder that pearls are merely one of many gifts from the sea, this shell pendant is engraved with images of the ocean's bounty. The pendant is paired with a simple strand of chocolate brown pearls surrounded by waves of seed beads and the necklace is fastened with a starfish toggle, clearly a trove of marine treasures.

MATERIALS

396 green Delicas
400 pewter size 11° seed beads
67 brown size 8° seed beads
12 green 4mm pearls
66 chocolate brown 6mm pearls
40mm shell pendant
Pewter toggle clasp
2 sterling silver 2mm crimp tubes
26" of .019 beading wire
Green Nymo size D beading thread

TOOLS

Scissors
Thread Heaven thread conditioner
Size 12 beading needle
Wire cutters
Crimping pliers
Bead stop

FINISHED SIZE

22½" (57 cm)

1 Place a bead stop on one end of the beading wire. String 1 size 8° seed bead and 1 chocolate brown pearl sixty-six times. String 1 size 8° and place a bead stop on the other end of the wire, leaving about ¼" of bare wire (to allow for movement when adding the seed beads).

2 Place a tension bead on one end of 3' of conditioned beading thread. Pass through the first size 8° strung. String 6 Delicas and pass through the next size 8°. Repeat sixty-five times. Tie a knot around the beading wire and repeat, passing back through the size 8° and string 6 pewter size 11°s between each. Pass back and forth through beads and knot several times to secure. Trim thread.

3 Remove 1 bead stop. String 1 size 11°, 1 crimp tube, 1 size 11°, and one half of the clasp. Pass back through the size 11° and crimp tube and crimp. Repeat for the other half of the necklace.

4 Use 6" of beading thread to string 1 green pearl, the pendant, and 11 green pearls. Pass through all beads again, forming a loop around the center of the necklace. Tie the thread ends together and trim.

Elizabeth I, The Pearl Queen

No historical figure of power and majesty had a more public passion for pearls than England's Elizabeth I, dubbed the "Pearl Queen." Her appetite for the lustrous gem was so intense that she owned more than 3,000 gowns in her lifetime that were decorated with pearls. To remove and re-embroider the pearls when garments were cleaned, Elizabeth employed a retinue of dressmakers and tailors. They also moved the pearls from one dress to another, since there were never sufficient pearls to cover all the dresses at one time. In her royal portraits, Elizabeth is always bejeweled, with pearls dominating her crowns, necklaces, earrings, and other jewelry. The pearl signified several important aspects of the powerful monarch who ruled England for forty-five years: the Virgin Queen's purity, her vast wealth and world power, and her love of luxurious beauty.

Queen Elizabeth I, attributed to George Gower circa 1588. National Portrait Gallery, London.

Wild Trellis

This very organic bracelet is a symbol of growth and regeneration. Top-drilled green pearls climbing the links of silver chain resemble little buds making their first appearance in the new, warmer season.

1 Cut the chain into two pieces. Use jump rings to attach the chains to each half of the clasp.

2 Use 3" of wire and 1 green pearl to form a wrapped loop bail that attaches to one of the circles on the chain. Repeat to attach 18 pearls to one piece of chain and 21 pearls to the other piece of chain.

MATERIALS

39 green 5x7mm top-drilled pearls
Sterling silver two-strand toggle clasp
4 sterling silver 6mm jump rings
13½" of sterling silver chain
117" of 24-gauge sterling silver wire

TOOLS

Wire cutters
Chain-nose pliers
Flat-nose pliers
Round-nose pliers

FINISHED SIZE

7½" (19 cm)

Center of Attention

Circles of chain broken up with wire-wrapped pink pearls lead to a centerpiece composed of more circles for a fun, flirty piece, perfect for a night out on the town.

MATERIALS

25 pink 5mm pearls

8 dark red 5mm pearls

4 sterling silver 11mm square Swiss cheese findings

2 sterling silver 13mm square Swiss cheese findings

1 sterling silver 15mm square Swiss cheese finding

1 sterling silver 6x16mm cage clasp

23" of sterling silver chain

11 sterling silver 24-gauge ball end head pins

44" of sterling silver 24-gauge wire

TOOLS

Wire cutters

Flat-nose pliers

Chain-nose pliers

Round-nose pliers

Nylon jaw pliers

FINISHED SIZE

21" (53.5 cm)

1 Use 2" of wire to form a wrapped loop that attaches to the top hole of one 11mm finding. String 1 pink pearl and form a wrapped loop that attaches to the top hole of one 13mm finding. Repeat to attach the 15mm finding, the second 13mm finding, and the second 11mm finding. Set aside.

2 Cut the chain into eight 2¼" pieces and four 1⅛" pieces.

3 Use 2" of wire to form a wrapped loop that attaches to one half of the clasp. String 1 pink pearl and form a wrapped loop that attaches to the top hole of one side of a third 11mm finding. Repeat for the other half of the clasp using the fourth 11mm finding.

4 Use 2" of wire to form a wrapped loop that attaches to the top hole of one of the two remaining 11mm findings to be used with the clasp. String 1 pearl and form a wrapped loop that attaches to 2¼" of chain. Use 2" of wire to form a wrapped loop that attaches to the other end of the chain. String 1 pink pearl and form a wrapped loop that attaches to 2¼" of chain. Use 2" of wire to form a wrapped loop that attaches to the other end of the chain. String 1 pink pearl and form a wrapped loop that attaches to 1⅛" of chain. Use 2" of wire to form a wrapped loop that attaches to the other end of chain. String 1 pink pearl and form a wrapped loop that attaches to the top hole of one of the 11mm findings used in Step 1.

5 Use 2" of wire to form a wrapped loop that attaches to the bottom hole of one of the 11mm findings used with the clasp. String 1 pearl and form a wrapped loop that attaches to 1⅛" of chain. Use 2" of wire to form a wrapped loop that attaches to the other end of the chain. String 1 pink pearl and form a wrapped loop that attaches to 2¼" of chain. Use 2" of wire to form a wrapped loop that attaches to the other end of the chain. String 1 pink pearl and form a wrapped loop that attaches to 2¼" of chain. Use 2" of wire to form a wrapped loop that attaches to the other end of chain. String 1 pink pearl and form a wrapped loop that attaches to the top hole of one of the 11mm findings used in Step 1.

6 Repeat Steps 3–5 for the other half of the necklace. Use 1 head pin to string 1 pink pearl. Form a wrapped loop that attaches to the bottom middle hole of the 15mm finding. Use 1 head pin to string 1 dark red pearl. Form a wrapped loop that attaches to the bottom left hole of the 15mm finding. Use 1 head pin to string 1 dark red pearl. Form a wrapped loop that attaches to the bottom right hole of the 15mm finding. Repeat entire step for each of the 13mm findings.

7 Use 1 head pin to string 1 dark red pearl. Form a wrapped loop that attaches to the bottom right hole of the 11mm finding. Repeat to attach a pearl to the bottom left hole of the other 11mm finding.

Brilliant Bangle

MATERIALS

18 transparent pearl chartreuse (DB124)
Delicas (A)

18 transparent silver-lined semi-matte
light jonquil (DB686) Delicas (B)

19 transparent pearl faded rose/gold
(DB102) Delicas (C)

19 metallic matte golden olive (DB371)
Delicas (D)

19 transparent matte AB dark amber
(DB853) Delicas (E)

19 transparent matte dark topaz (DB764)
Delicas (F)

16 color-lined amber/dark amber
(DB287) Delicas (G)

18 lime 4mm pearls

19 taupe 4mm pearls

19 rust 4mm pearls

8 sterling silver 2mm cornerless cubes

64 silver head pins

Sterling silver 2¹/₂" bangle bracelet with
loops

TOOLS

Flat-nose pliers

Round-nose pliers

Chain-nose pliers

Wire cutters

FINISHED SIZE

3¹/₂" (9 cm)

Six colors of seed beads blend to bring out the glow and nuance of each of three colors of pearls. The addition of tiny silver accents adds extra sparkle to this dazzling creation.

1 Use a head pin to string 1A, 1 lime pearl, and 1B. Repeat for a total of 18 lime head pins.

2 Use a head pin to string 1C, 1 taupe pearl, and 1D. Repeat for a total of 19 taupe head pins.

3 Use a head pin to string 1E, 1 rust pearl, and 1F. Repeat for a total of 19 rust head pins.

4 Use a head pin to string 1G, 1 cornerless cube, and 1G. Repeat for a total of 8 cornerless cube head pins.

5 Use 1 lime head pin to form a wrapped loop that attaches to one loop of the bangle. Repeat, using 1 taupe head pin on the next loop of the bangle. Repeat, using 1 rust head pin on the next loop of the bangle. Repeat entire step for the circumference of the bangle.

6 Use 1 cornerless cube head pin to form a wrapped loop that attaches to any loop of the bangle. Repeat, placing 1 cornerless cube head pin every seven loops of the bangle.

TINY GEMS:

In 1887, the French government auctioned off a substantial collection of the French royal jewels in order to bolster the country's sagging treasury. A number of the pearl pieces that were purchased by jewelers and collectors were later broken apart and redesigned.

Very Berry

Tiny pink pearls stitched into berrylike clusters are the impetus for these "oh so very" dangling chain earrings.

MATERIALS

70 dark pink 3mm potato pearls
Sterling silver ear wires with five loops
9½" of sterling silver chain
10 sterling silver head pins
20" of 24-gauge sterling silver wire
Dark pink Nymo size D beading thread

TOOLS

Scissors
Thread Heaven thread conditioner
Size 12 beading needle
Wire cutters
Flat-nose pliers
Chain-nose pliers
Round-nose pliers

FINISHED SIZE

3" (7.5 cm)

1 Use 8" of conditioned thread to string 4 pearls, leaving a 3" tail. Pass through all pearls again to form a loop. Secure with a square knot. Pass through the first pearl strung, string 1 pearl, and pass back through the third pearl strung (Figure 1). Pass through the fourth pearl strung, string 1 pearl, and pass back through the second pearl strung. Pass through all pearls again to secure. Use the tail and working threads to tie a surgeon's knot. Trim threads. Repeat for a total of ten pearl balls.

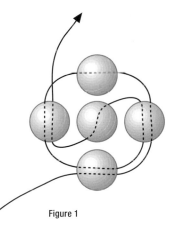

Figure 1

2 Cut the chain into four ¾" pieces, four 1" pieces, and two 1¼" pieces.

3 Use 1 head pin to string 1 pearl ball and form a wrapped loop that attaches to one end of one piece of chain. Repeat for all pieces of chain.

4 Use 2" of wire to form a wrapped loop that attaches to the first hole of one ear wire. String 1 pearl and form a wrapped loop that attaches to the other end of a ¾" piece of chain. Repeat to attach a 1" piece of chain, 1¼" piece of chain, 1" piece of chain, and ¾" piece of chain to the ear wire. Repeat entire step for the other earring.

did you know . . .

The Add-A-Pearl Necklace

Generations of young girls have received the gift that keeps on growing—an Add-A-Pearl starter necklace. The necklace begins as a 14-karat gold chain with a single pearl (either cultured or natural). As time passes, additional pearls are given to the girl to celebrate special occasions such as birthdays, holidays, or anniversaries. In time, the necklace becomes a complete strand of pearls.

THE Add-a-pearl NECKLACE
GENUINE ORIENTAL PEARLS

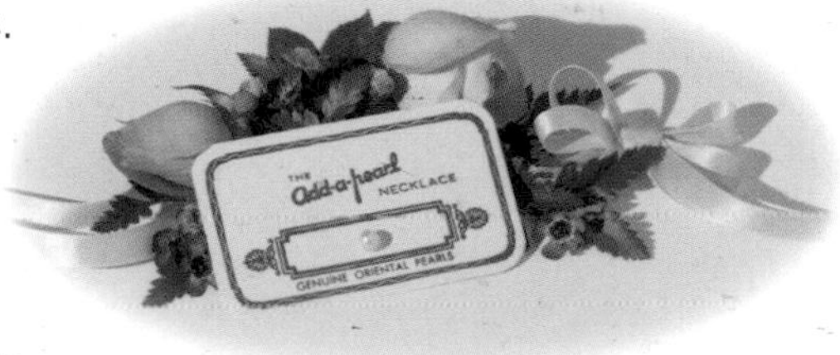

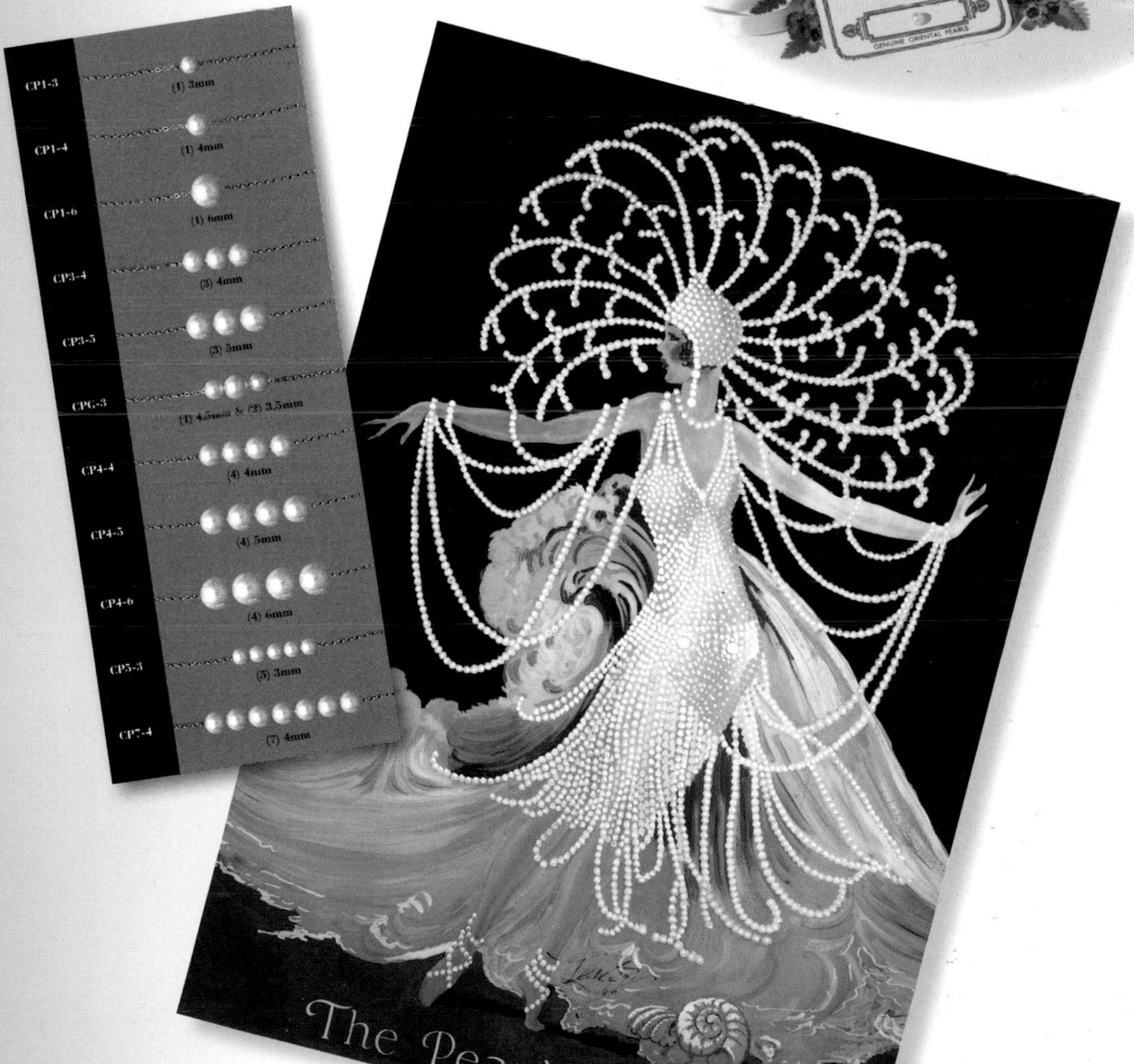

CP1-3
(1) 3mm
CP1-4
(1) 4mm
CP1-6
(1) 6mm
CP3-4
(3) 4mm
CP3-5
(3) 5mm
CPG-3
(1) 4.5mm & (2) 3.5mm
CP4-4
(4) 4mm
CP4-5
(4) 5mm
CP4-6
(4) 6mm
CP5-3
(5) 3mm
CP7-4
(7) 4mm
The Pearl Girl

techniques
and findings

TECHNIQUES

Crimping

Crimp tubes

Crimp tubes are seamless tubes of metal that come in several sizes. To use, string a crimp tube through the connection finding. Pass back through the tube, leaving a short tail. Use the back notch of the crimping pliers to press the length of the tube down between the wires, enclosing them in separate chambers of the crescent shape. Rotate the tube 90° and use the front notch of the pliers to fold the two chambers onto themselves, forming a clean cylinder. Trim the excess wire.

Crimp covers

Crimp covers hide a 2mm crimp tube and give a professional finish. To attach, gently hold a crimp cover in the front notch of the crimping pliers. Insert the crimped tube and gently squeeze the pliers, encasing the tube inside the cover.

Twisted crimps

Twisted crimps are crimp tubes that have been "twisted," creating ridges on the inside of the tube that grip beading wire. Crimp beads are serrated metal beads. Twisted crimps and crimp beads can be secured by squeezing them flat with chain- or flat-nose pliers.

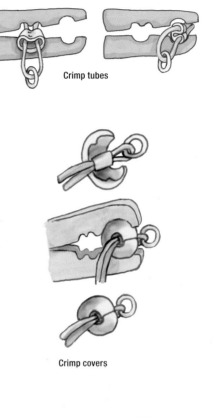

Crimp tubes

Crimp covers

Twisted crimp

Gluing

Place a sparing amount of glue on knots to secure them (we recommend G-S Hypo Cement or clear nail polish), or use enough glue to completely secure beads to a surface (E6000, Terrifically Tacky Tape). Allow any glue to dry thoroughly before continuing.

Knots

Half hitch knot

Half hitch knot

Half hitch knots may be worked with two or more strands—one strand is knotted over one or more other strands. Form a loop around the cord(s). Pull the end through the loop just formed and pull tight. Repeat for the length of cord you want to cover.

Overhand knot

The overhand knot is the basic knot for tying off thread. Make a loop with the stringing material. Pass the cord that lies behind the loop over the front cord and through the loop. Pull tight.

Square knot

Square knot

The square knot is the classic sturdy knot for securing most stringing materials. First make an overhand knot, passing the right end over the left end. Next, make another overhand knot, this time passing the left end over the right end. Pull tight.

Surgeon's knot

Surgeon's knot

The surgeon's knot is very secure and therefore good for finishing off most stringing materials. Tie an overhand knot, right over left, but instead of one twist over the left cord, make at least two. Tie another overhand knot, left over right, and pull tight.

Finishing and Starting New Threads

Tie off your old thread when it's about 4" long by making a simple knot between beads. Pass through a few beads and pull tight to hide the knot. Weave through a few more beads and trim the thread close to the work. Start the new thread by tying a knot between beads and weaving through a few beads. Pull tight to hide the knot. Weave through several beads until you reach the place to resume beading.

Pass Through vs Pass Back Through

"Pass through" means to move your needle in the same direction that the beads have been strung. "Pass back through" means to move your needle in the opposite direction.

Pearl Knotting

Pearl knotting is traditionally done with silk thread, placing a knot between each bead to prevent them from rubbing against each other. Gently pre-stretch the silk by pulling it inch by inch through your thumb and forefinger. Silk thread generally comes with a needle attached. Use this needle to string a bead, then form a loose overhand knot. Place the needle, or an awl or tweezers, in the knot and hold it next to the bead. Gently pull the thread to tighten the knot around the needle, then pull the needle back out of the knot.

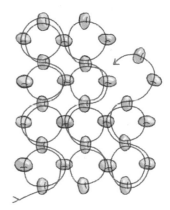

Pearl knotting

Right-Angle Weave (Single Needle)

String 4 beads and pass through them again to form the first unit. For the rest of the row, string 3 beads, pass through the last bead passed through in the previous unit, and the first 2 just strung; the thread path will resemble a figure eight, alternating directions with each unit. To begin the next row, pass through the last 3 beads strung to exit the side of the last unit. String 3 beads, pass through the last bead passed through, and the first bead just strung. *String 2 beads, pass through the next edge bead of the previous row, the last bead passed through in the previous unit, and the last 2 beads just strung. Pass through the next edge bead of the previous row, string 2 beads, pass through the last bead of the previous unit, the edge bead just passed through, and the first bead just strung. Repeat from * to complete the row, then begin a new row as before.

Right-angle weave

Stringing

Stringing is a technique in which you use a beading wire, needle and thread, or other material to gather beads into a strand.

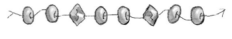

Stringing

Tension Bead

String a bead larger than those you are working with, then pass through the bead one or more times, making sure not to split your thread. The bead will be able to slide along but will still provide tension to work against when you're beading the first two rows.

Tension bead

Tubular Peyote Stitch

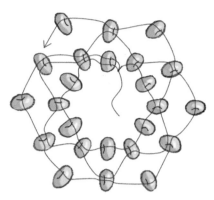

Tubular peyote stitch

String an even number of beads and make a foundation circle by passing through them two more times, exiting from the first bead strung. String 1 bead and pass through the third bead of the foundation circle. String 1 bead and pass through the fifth bead of the foundation circle. Continue adding 1 bead at a time, skipping over 1 bead of the first round, until you have added half the number of beads of the first round. Exit from the first bead of the second round. String 1 bead, pass through the second bead added in the second round, and pull thread tight. String 1 bead and pass through the third bead added in the second round. Continue around, filling in the "spaces" 1 bead at a time. Exit from the first bead added in each round.

Wireworking

Wireworking

To form a wrapped loop, begin with a 90° bend at least 2" from the end of the wire. Use round-nose pliers to form a simple loop with a tail overlapping the bend. Wrap the tail tightly down the neck of the wire to create a couple of coils. Trim the excess wire to finish. Make a heavier-looking, double wrapped loop by wrapping the wire back up over the coils, toward the loop, and trimming at the loop.

Cones, Dangles, Wrapped Bails

Cones

Cones

Use cones to finish a multistrand piece. Attach each strand of beads to a wrapped loop or an eye pin. Use the wrapped-loop wire to string the wide end of a cone, covering the ends of the stringing material. Form a wrapped loop at the tip of the cone that attaches to a clasp.

Dangles

Dangles can be strung as they are, attached using jump rings, or linked onto other loops. Use a head pin or eye pin to string the bead(s), then form a simple or wrapped loop.

Wrapped Bails

Wrapped bails turn top-drilled beads, usually teardrops, into pendants. Center the bead on a 6" piece of wire. Bend both ends of the wire up the sides and across the top of the bead. Bend one end straight up at the center of the bead and wrap the other wire around it to form a few coils. Form a wrapped loop with the straight-up wire, wrapping it back down over the already-formed coils. Trim the excess wire.

French Wire

French wire is a fine coil of wire strung at the connection between the beaded strand and a finding. String ¼" or so of French wire after you've strung the crimp tube, then string the clasp.

Head Pins

Head pins are straight wires with a ball or flat disc at one end. Eye pins are straight wires that end in a simple loop.

Jump Rings

Jump rings connect holes and loops. Open a jump ring by grasping each side of its opening with a pair of pliers. Don't pull apart. Instead, twist in opposite directions so that you can open and close without distorting the shape.

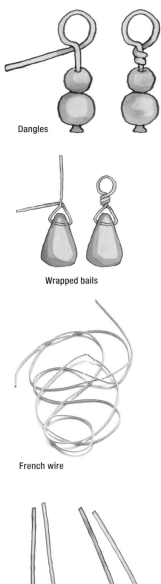

Dangles

Wrapped bails

French wire

Head pins

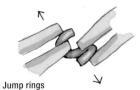

Jump rings

RELATED READING

Campbell, Jean. *Stringing Style 2.* Loveland, Colorado: Interweave Press, 2007.

Durant, Judith, and Jean Campbell. *The Beader's Companion.* Loveland, Colorado: Interweave Press, 2005.

Hackney, Ki, and Diana Edkins. *People & Pearls: The Magic Endures.* New York: Harper Collins Publishers, 2000.

Hogsett, Jamie. *Stringing Style.* Loveland, Colorado: Interweave Press, 2005.

Kunz, George Frederick, and Charles Hugh Stevenson. *The Book of the Pearl: Its History, Art, Science and Industry.* New York: Dover Publications Inc., 1993. First published in 1908 by The Century Co.

Landman, Neil H., Paula Mikkelsen, Rüdiger Bieler, and Bennet Bronson. *Pearls: A Natural History.* New York: Harry N. Abrams, 2001.

Miller, Andy. *Cultured Pearls: The First Hundred Years.* Lausanne, Switzerland: Golay Buchel Group, 1997.

For more beading designs and techniques, join the community at beadingdaily.com, where life meets beading, or subscribe to Interweave's beading magazines:

Beadwork
Jewelry Artist
Step by Step Beads
Step by Step Wire Jewelry
Stringing

PROJECT RESOURCES

Materials:

Classic Pearl Knotting, p. 18
Swarovski crystal pearls, clasps, Griffin Silk Bead Cord, and French wire: Fusion Beads
Pearls: Fire Mountain Gems

Purple Pearls, p. 22
All Swarovski beads: Fusion Beads

Dark Beauties, p. 24
Bead Bumpers: Beadalon
Pearls and strand separator: Fusion Beads

Coin of the Realm, p. 26
Coin pearls and 14k findings: The Bead Shop

Mother-of-Pearl Radiance, p. 28
All materials: Fire Mountain Gems and Beads

The Midas Touch, p. 32
Pearls: Fire Mountain Gems and Beads
Spacers: Bead Cache
Clasp: Rishashay

Cuff Deluxe, p. 36
Clasp: The Bead Shop
Pearls: Lucky Gems

Champagne Necklace, p. 44
Ribbon: Oak Grove Yarn, Desert Sand colorway
Pearls: Ayla's Originals
Clasp and cones: Pacific Silverworks

Sacred Vows Lariat, p. 48
Pearls: The Bead Shop
Links: Fusion Beads

Lavender Bouquet, p. 52
All materials: Fusion Beads

Pearl Fusion, p. 58
Clasp: Saki Silver
Pendant: Diane Hawkey
Chain: Fusion Beads
Cornerless cubes: Kamol

Copper Romance, p. 62
Swarovski crystal pearls: Fusion Beads
Clasp: The Bead Shop

Midnight Tassel, p. 66
Pearls and jump rings: The Bead Shop
Clasp: Fusion Beads

Chain Reaction, p. 74
Black pearls: The Bead Shop
White pearls: Fire Mountain Gems and Beads
Teal pearls, clasp, and chain: Fusion Beads
Jump rings: Via Murano

Global Pearls, p. 78
Teal pearls: Pearl Concepts
Gold pearls: Lucky Gems
Copper pearls: Austin Gem & Bead
Polymer rounds: Heather Wynn

Catch of the Day, p. 82
Charms and clasp: Rishashay
C-Lon Bead Cord: Jane's Fiber and Beads

Off the Grid, p. 86
Pearls: Fusion Beads

Ocean Wonders, p. 92
Pendant: Lillypilly Designs
Clasp: Green Girl Studios
Pearls: Fusion Beads
Seed beads: Bead Cache

Wild Trellis, p. 96
Pearls and clasp: Fusion Beads
Chain: The Bead Shop
Jump rings: Via Murano

Center of Attention, p. 98
All materials: Fusion Beads

Brilliant Bangle, p. 102
Pearls and bangle bracelet: Fusion Beads
Delicas: Bead Cache

Very Berry, p. 106
Ear wires and head pins: The Bead Shop
Chain and pearls: Fusion Beads

Sources:

Ayla's Originals
1511 Sherman Ave.
Evanston, IL 60201
(877) 328-AYLA
www.aylasoriginals.com

Beadalon
440 Highlands Blvd.
Coatesville, PA 19320 USA
(866) 4BEADALON (423-2325)
www.beadalon.com

Bead Cache
3307 South College Ave., Ste. 105
Fort Collins, CO 80525
(970) 224-4322

The Bead Shop
158 University Ave.
Palo Alto, CA 94301
(650) 328-7925
www.beadshop.com

Fire Mountain Gems and Beads
(800) 355-2137
www.firemountaingems.com

Fusion Beads
3830 Stone Wy. North
Seattle, WA 98103
(888) 781-3559
www.fusionbeads.com

Green Girl Studios
PO Box 19389
Asheville, NC 28815
(828) 298-2263
www.greengirlstudios.com

Diane Hawkey
(248) 541-0211
www.dianehawkey.com

Jane's Fiber and Beads
5415 East Andrew Johnson Hwy.
PO Box 110
Afton, TN 37616
(888) 497-2665
www.janesfiberandbeads.com

Kamol
(206) 764-7375
kamolbeads@yahoo.com

Lillypilly Designs
PO Box 270136
Louisville, CO 80027
(303) 543-8673
www.lillypillydesigns.com

Lucky Gems
1220 Broadway, 3/F
New York, NY 10001
(212) 268-8866
www.lucky-gems.com

Pacific Silverworks
461 E. Main St., Ste. A
Ventura, CA 93001
(805) 641-1394
www.pacificsilverworks.com

Rishashay
PO Box 8271
Missoula, MT 59807
(800) 517-3311
www.rishashay.com

Saki Silver
362 Ludlow Ave.
Cincinnati, OH 45220
(513) 861-9626
www.sakisilver.com

Via Murano
17654 Newhope St., Ste. A
Fountain Valley, CA 92708
(877) VIAMURANO

Heather Wynn
PO Box 6474
Gulf Breeze, FL 32563
www.heatherwynn.com

INDEX

Add-A-Pearl Necklace 109
Akoya 40, 57
aragonite 9

bails, wrapped 115
baroque 13, 47
bead, tension 113
bibliography 116
Biwa 13
blister pearls 61
Breakfast at Tiffany's 65
Buddha pearls 61
button pearls 13

Caesar, Julius 71
calcium carbonate 9
care of pearls 12
Chanel, Gabrielle ("Coco")
 47, 65
cleaning 12
Cleopatra 70
color 12, 57; dyed 12
Columbus 81
conchiolin 9
cones 114
crimping 111
crimp covers 111
crimp tubes 111
crimps, twisted 111
Croft, Henry 31
cultured pearls 9, 13, 41, 57, 61

da Vinci, Leonardo 47
dangles 115
dog collars 11, 35

E6000 111
Elizabeth I 47, 95
essence d'orient 47
fashion 65
French wire 115
freshwater pearls 13, 40, 61, 91

glue 111
Great Age of Pearls 81
G-S Hypo Cement 111

half hitch knot 112
Haskell, Miriam 47
head pins 115
Hepburn, Audrey 65

imitation pearls 47

Jacquin 47
jump rings 115

Keshi 13
knots 112
knotting, pearl 113

lengths, necklace 11
Linnaeus 57
luster 9, 11

Mikimoto, Kokichi 57
Mise, Tatsuhei 57
Mississippi River 91
mother-of-pearl 9, 31, 40, 47, 91

nacre 9, 40, 61
Nishikawa, Dr. Tokichi 57
natural pearls 9
necklace lengths 11
nucleus 9

Onassis, Jacqueline Kennedy 65
oval pearls 13
overhand knot 112

pass back through 112
pass through 112
Pearl Coast 81
pearl knotting 113
Pearlies of London 31
Peregrina, La 70
peyote stitch, tubular 114
Pinctada fucata 40
Pinctada margaritifera 40
Pinctada maxima 40
Pliny the Elder 70
poppyseed pearls 13
Princess Diana 65
Princess Grace Kelly 65

Queen Alexandra 35

restringing 12
resources 117–118
rice crispies 13
right-angle weave 113
Roman Empire 71
round pearls 13

saltwater pearls 11, 40
sea pearls 40
shape 12, 13
size 12
square knot 112
stick pearls 13
storage 12
stringing 12, 113
Suetonius 71
surface 11
surgeon's knot 112

Taylor, Elizabeth 70
techniques 111–115
tension bead 113
Terrifically Tacky Tape 111
The Incomparable 70
thread, starting and finishing
 112
tooth test 47
tubular peyote stitch 114
twisted crimps 111

Venus 71
von Linné, Carl 57

wedding pearls 43, 51
wire, French 115
wireworking 114
wrapped bails 115